THE
HIBERNIAN
FC
MISCELLANY

BOBBY SINNET

The
History
Press

For Elliot & Mairi

First published in 2012 by

The History Press
The Mill, Brimscombe Port
Stroud, Gloucestershire, GL5 2QG
www.thehistorypress.co.uk

British Library Cataloguing in Publication Data.
A catalogue record for this book is available from the British Library.

ISBN 978 0 7524 6473 2

Typesetting and origination by The History Press
Printed in Great Britain

FOREWORD

By Gordon Rae

I was honoured to be asked to write the foreword for this book on Hibernian, as there is no doubt that the club will always have a place in my heart. It is the club where I began my career and undoubtedly helped me to get to where I am today.

I was delighted to be picked up by Hibernian under the management of 'Famous Five' legend Eddie Turnbull, for whom I had the utmost respect, and still have. I always think players can be prouder when they play for their local club – which unfortunately happens less and less nowadays – but that was certainly true of myself every time I pulled on the green and white sleeved shirt of Hibernian FC.

I was fortunate that during my time at Hibernian FC I was able to play with and meet lots of great players, fans and individuals. All of these wonderful people have one thing in common – a great love and high regard for the Hibees. Many of them have become lifelong friends. They are all part of the Hibernian story.

I made my debut as a forward in a 2–1 defeat at home to Queen of the South in the League Cup, but my second appearance just three days later was more successful – I scored in a 2–0 win against Rangers at Ibrox. I benefitted from the experience of players around me like Des Bremner, who would win the European Cup with Aston Villia in 1982, and John Blackley who had played for Scotland in the 1974 World Cup. Later in my career I would play in front of Scotland goalkeeper Andy Goram, and alongside Scotland internationals Steve Archibald and John Collins. There were some great days at Hibs, and beating Aberdeen to make the Scottish Cup final in 1979 was definitely up there with the best, especially as I scored that night. We were so dreadfully unlucky not to win that final against Rangers after three games, but it was not to be.

In the later years of my Hibs career we had an excellent team and it was an exciting time to be at Easter Road as experienced internationals like Steve Archibald played alongside local boys like Paul Kane and Micky Weir. We also turned the tables on our local rivals and enjoyed some excellent derby results at this time – I'm proud to say I played my part.

After 13 years it was hard to leave Easter Road, and end my playing career with Partick Thistle, Hamilton Academical and Meadowbank Thistle. I did return later as a coach, and I was pleased to see some of my boys go on to become first-team regulars. I still follow the Hibs results, and try to get to see them whenever I am home.

This book details many stories about what is really one of the biggest clubs in Scottish football, and many of the tales will, I hope, both surprise and entertain you. I hope you find it as enjoyable as I did.

Gordon Rae, 2012

INTRODUCTION

Writing this book about Hibernian has been a real labour of love, as they are my club, and have been for over 25 years. I started collecting Hibernian programmes, before moving on to collating statistics and spending hours in libraries researching the rich tapestry of Hibs history. There are many stories to tell about the club which has been an integral and important part of Leith and Edinburgh for over 135 years now.

It's not a complete history of the club, but tries to cover all facets of its life and times through the years and all statistics are correct up to the end of the 2011/12 season. Hopefully it will be a good read and prompt many 'I never knew that' moments as the information is digested.

I would like to thank my wife Claire for her support and encouragement, Thomas Jamieson for his statistical help, my mum and dad, Richard Leatherdale from The History Press for his incredible patience, Gordon Rae for the foreword, and as a point of reference, the *Scotsman* and *Edinburgh News*, as well as the books on the club by among others John R. Mackay, Tom Wright and Alan Lugton. I'd also like to express my appreciation to Iain Murray for getting me this gig, and to fellow Hibby cohorts Sean Allan, Dale Crease and Alasdair Oliphant.

Let's hope that under Pat Fenlon we will soon have more silverware to add to the text.

IN THE BEGINNING

On 6 August 1875 the Catholic Young Men's Society of St Patrick's Church in the Cowgate area of Edinburgh formed its own football club, a game that was becoming more and more popular. Canon Edward Joseph Hannon saw this as an opportunity to help the members of his church integrate into the wider Edinburgh community – a problem that had been an issue ever since the Irish had started to migrate to Edinburgh and particularly after the Potato famine earlier in the nineteenth century.

Choosing a name was slightly less straightforward, and several options were considered before the name 'Hibernian' was decided upon. Hibernia was the Latin name for Ireland, and this was fitting as the team were entirely Irish-born with the exception of one player, who of course had Irish parents.

Hibs struggled to gain acceptance from the Scottish and Edinburgh footballing authorities of the time, and indeed other clubs were instructed not to play them. However, Heart of Midlothian were Hibs' first opponents on Christmas Day 1875, and other teams followed on, Hibernian eventually being admitted to both the Edinburgh and Scottish Football Associations.

From humble beginnings they entered the Scottish Cup for the first time in 1877 and 10 years later, in 1887, became the first team from the east to win the Scottish Cup, cementing their place as the premier side of Edinburgh. They became founder members of the Scottish Second Division in 1893, were promoted to the top league in 1895 and, barring the odd mishap, have remained there to this day.

OTHER TEAMS WITH THE HIBS NAME

The most famous of all the other 'Hibs' is Hibernians FC of Malta but there seems to be little connection between the two clubs.

In Hibernian's early years they were instrumental in helping set up many teams, and all the following teams carried the Hibernian name – there's some surprising names where you wouldn't expect to find a Hibs team now:

Arbroath Hibernian
Brechin Hibernian
Cowal Hibernian
Kilmarnock Hibernian
St Josephs Hibernian
Kimaurs Hibernian
Alloa Hibernian
Bonhill Hibernian
Yoker Hibernian
Smithston Hibernian
Dumbarton Hibernian
Duntocher Hibernian
Milngavie Hibernian
Dundee Hibernian
Lochee Hibernian
Dunfermline Hibernian
Fifeshire Hibernian
Thornton Hibernian
Glasgow Hibernian
League Hibernian
Tollcross Hibernian
Govan Hibernian
Eastern Hibernian
Parkhead Hibernian

Western Hibernian
Airdrie Hibernian
Clarkston Hibernian
Blantyre Hibernian
Cambuslang Hibernian
Cambuslang Hibernian Juniors
Chapelhall Hibernian
Coatbridge Hibernian
Coatdyke Hibernian
Larkhall Hibernian
Mossend Hibernian
Motherwell Hibernian
Tannochside Hibernian
Wishaw Hibernian
Peebles Hibernian
Greenock Hibernian
Johnstone Hibernian
Paisley Hibernian
Denny Hibernian
Falkirk Hibernian
Fauldhouse Hibernian
Queensferry Hibernian
Maryhill Hibernian

Thornton Hibs are one of the few sides that exist to this day, playing their football in the East Region Central Division.

Dundee Hibernian also still exist to this day, but no longer carry the Hibernian name – they changed it to United in 1923 in an attempt to give the club wider appeal. At the same time they dropped their green jerseys in favour of black and white colours, which they later changed to their well-known tangerine kits.

SCORING IN CONSECUTIVE GAMES

Back in October 1959, Joe Baker started a run of 10 league games where he scored in every game. The games were as follows (Hibs score first):

17 Oct	H	Dunfermline Athletic	7–4	(3)
24 Oct	A	Airdrieonians	11–1	(3)
31 Oct	H	Celtic	3–3	(2)
7 Nov	A	St Mirren	3–2	(1)
14 Nov	A	Raith Rovers	2–4	(1)
21 Nov	H	Dundee	4–2	(2)
28 Nov	H	Stirling Albion	3–1	(2)
5 Dec	A	Arbroath	3–2	(3)
12 Dec	H	Ayr United	5–1	(1)
19 Dec	A	Partick Thistle	10–2	(2)

The run came to an end when Joe failed to score on Boxing Day when Hibs lost 6–4 to Aberdeen at Pittodrie. The run had seen the club move from tenth in an 18-team league up to third. In the ten games Hibs had won 8, drawn 1 and lost 1, scoring 51 goals in the process while conceding 22. Joe had helped himself to 3 hat-tricks and 3 doubles for a total of 20. The away victories against Airdrie and Partick Thistle remain the only times that Hibs have scored 10 or more in a league game away from home.

100 GOALS IN A SEASON

In 1959/60 Hibernian managed for the first and so far only time to score 100 league goals in a season when they managed 106, more than champions Hearts and every other team in the league. Unfortunately their defence was as prone to letting them in and 85 goals were conceded, which meant that Hibs finished the season in a mid-table seventh position.

MOST GOALS IN A SEASON

In 1952/53 Hibs scored a whopping 147 goals in all competitions. The goals were shared out among the 'Famous Five' and Bobby Combe; Lawrie Reilly scored 46, Eddie Turnbull 25, Bobby Johnstone 23, Gordon Smith 20, Willie Ormond 18 and Bobby Combe 12. In addition, Jimmy Souness, Willie Clark and Archie Buchanan chipped in with a goal each. Hibs finished second in the league, reached the semi-final of the League Cup and the quarter-final of the Scottish Cup. The also made the final of the Coronation Cup where they lost to a Jock Stein-inspired Celtic while being hot favourites.

COLOURS

Hibs colours are famous – the green shirts with white sleeves, are as iconic as they are well known. These weren't the original colours of the team, though; when they were formed in 1875 they chose white jerseys as their team colours. This changed to green and white hooped jerseys in 1876, a full 12 years before Celtic were formed. In 1879 this changed again to an all-green jersey, and this was to remain the club's colours up until 1938, when the white sleeves were introduced. There are conflicting theories as to why it was changed, with some believing the Arsenal kit to be an inspiration.

Hibs wore the distinctive white-sleeved kit for the first time on 13 August 1938 at Easter Road in a league game against Hamilton Academical before a crowd of 20,000. The Hibs team that day was Archie Gourlay, David Logan, Alexander Prior, Charles Birse, James Miller, William Rice, Bobby Nutley, Willie Finnegan, Arthur Milne, Patrick Harte and Timothy O'Keefe. The game finished 2–2, and Patrick Harte grabbed both the Hibs goals.

MOVIE STARS

A couple of former Hibs players have appeared in movies. *The Acid House* was a film based on the book of the same name by novelist and Hibs fan Irvine Welsh. In the segment the 'Granton Star Cause', the barman is played by Hibs' centenary captain Pat Stanton.

Andy McLaren was a Scottish international who had a spell at Hibs as a trialist under Bobby Williamson. The spell ended in acrimony when he wasn't offered a contract. In 2012 he had an uncredited and non-speaking part in the Ken Loach film *The Angels' Share*, where he played the part of the father of a victim of violence.

SPONSORS

Hibs were among the first sides in the UK to embrace shirt sponsorship when they signed a deal with sports manufacturer Bukta to display the company's name on the front of their jerseys. In later years Hibs would be sponsored by Fishers Garage, Insave, P&D Windows and the Frank Graham Group. After those sponsors, Hibs had a single season where they did not carry a shirt sponsor in 1991/92 – this season saw the Skol Cup victory.

Since then, Hibs have been sponsored by Macbean Protective Clothing, energy supplier Calor Gas, brewing giant Carlsberg, whisky distiller Whyte & Mackay and property investment specialists McEwan Fraser. Current sponsors are alcoholic ginger beer manufacturers Crabbies who have a deal that runs until 2014.

Due to European restrictions on the promotion of alcohol, Hibs have used a number of different sponsors in some recent European games. In 2004, the shirt carried the Whyte & Mackay blue shield logo, without any lettering. In 2005 and 2006 brewers Carling had their name on the jerseys, and in 2008 against Swedish team Elfsborg, the shirts were sponsored by the Hibernian Community Foundation.

TALLEST

Hibernian's League Cup-winning captain Rob Jones is the club's tallest recorded player, coming in at a whopping 6ft 7in. The central defender and former schoolteacher, who also served as a centre forward when required, joined Hibs from Stockport County in 2006. Rob was to be a fixture in the centre of the Hibs defence for the next three years racking up 118 appearances and scoring 13 goals, including the opener in the League Cup final against Kilmarnock in 2007. He also scored the winner that season against Hearts at Easter Road in the quarter-final in a 1–0 victory. He moved on to Scunthorpe for what was for Scunthorpe a club record fee, before joining Sheffield Wednesday.

SMALLEST

By contrast the smallest recorded Hibs player was Johnny Grant, not to be confused with John Grant who played in the same season. Johnny was just 5ft 3in and only played for one season having joined the club in 1963 and making 13 appearances and scoring a single goal. He joined Hibs from Kilwinning Rangers having previously played for Queen's Park. Grant moved on to Ayr United in 1965, and emigrated to South Africa after being released from the Somerset Park side.

Micky Weir was marginally bigger at 5ft 4in. He was a Skol Cup winner with Hibs in 1991, making 247 appearances between 1983 and 1996. He scored 35 goals, including one headed effort against Dunfermline. Upon leaving Hibs he moved on to Motherwell.

LEGENDS – GORDON SMITH

Gordon Smith is considered by many to be the finest footballer ever to wear the green and white of Hibernian. He was born in Edinburgh, but at a young age he moved to Montrose. He excelled as a schoolboy, and played for Montrose Roselea and Dundee North End, winning schoolboy honours.

He was offered a trial for his boyhood heroes Heart of Midlothian, but the then Hibs manager Willie McCartney stepped in and snapped up the 16-year-old from under the noses of the Edinburgh rivals. Apparently it caused quite a shock when Gordon lined up to make his debut in April 1941 in a wartime league game against Hearts! What happened next is scarcely believable but set the tone for a great career in green and white and the following years – Hibs won 5–3, and the youngster helped himself to a hat-trick! He only just missed out on being a part of the team that lifted the Summer Cup in 1941, with Caskie being preferred to the youngster.

Smith was to enjoy considerable success as a Hibs player, and earned the nickname 'the gay gordon'. He was an integral part of the three championship winning sides, as well as the Southern League Cup winning team in 1944, scoring an incredible number of goals for a winger.

He scored his last Hibs goal in a game against Raith Rovers on 31 January 1959 and made his final appearance against Third Lanark in March 1959 in a 2–1 defeat. Although he had played predominantly as a right winger, his career at Hibs ended as it had begun – as a centre forward.

When Hibs released him at the age of 35 after a persistent ankle problem, many considered that would be the end of Smith's career but not the great man himself and he signed on at Hearts for a couple of years where he won another league title, and a League Cup medal. When Hearts released him after an injury-hit second season, not many expected him to carry on but he moved on to Dundee where he struck up an excellent understanding with a young Hibs fan called Alan Gilzean who was also an accomplished centre forward. They led Dundee to their only league title in 1962, and Gordon once again found himself playing in the European Cup at the age of 38. This campaign included an 8–1 victory before they lost to AC Milan.

Altogether, Smith won 5 league titles and 1 League Cup. As with so many of his contemporaries, the Scottish Cup eluded him. He was an initial inductee to the Hibernian FC Hall of Fame.

He played 636 competitive games for Hibs, scoring 303 goals. He won 19 Scotland caps between 1946 and 1957, captaining the side on 4 occasions. He sadly died in 2004.

KIT MANUFACTURERS

Hibs' current kit manufacturer is Puma, who are contracted until 2013. The list of previous kit manufacturers is as follows:

1977–80	Bukta
1980–7	Umbro
1987–92	Adidas
1992–4	Bukta
1994–8	Mitre
1998–2010	Le Coq Sportif
2010–	Puma

HOME FROM HOME

Hibs started the 1924/25 season at Tynecastle while the club constructed the new Main Stand. The stand was to remain in place until 2001, when it was knocked down and replaced by the new West Stand.

Hibs played two games on Friday nights at Tynecastle, which both ended in victories. The first was against Partick Thistle on 15 August 1924, and Hibs won 3–2 with a team consisting of Willie Harper, William McGinnigle, William Dornan, Peter Kerr, Willie Miller, Hugh Shaw, Harry Ritchie, Jimmy Dunn, Jimmy McColl, Johnny Halligan and John Walker. Jimmy Dunn scored twice, and Jimmy McColl notched the other in front of a crowd of 18,000.

The second Tynecastle match was against Kilmarnock on 29 August 1924, and Hibs won 1–0. The side was unchanged from the Partick Thistle game a fortnight earlier and the goal was scored by Jimmy McColl, Hibs recording their third straight win at the start of the season to go second in the league. Hugh Shaw featured in both games, and of course went on to manage Hibs to their three league championships in the post-war era.

These weren't the only occasions that Hibs played away from home. Back in 1904, Hibs chose to play a home game at Hampden due to 'competing attractions' in Edinburgh. At the beginning of the last century Hibs still had a large following in Glasgow, so the decision to move the game to Hampden wasn't as surprising as it might seem now. Hibs lost 3–1 to Queen's Park in front of 3,000, John Divers scoring their goal. The team that day on 13 February was: Rennie, Gray, Glen, Harrower, Maconnachie, Buchan, Campbell, McGeachan, Divers, Callaghan and Stewart.

Hearts have on occasion also used their Edinburgh Derby rivals' ground for a home game – back in 1914 they defeated Raith Rovers 2–0 at Easter Road. Bizarrely, St Mirren used Easter Road for a home fixture against Hearts in 1921. It did not do the Paisley side much good as they crashed to a 4–0 defeat.

... AND HOME FROM AWAY

Conversely, Hibs have also played away from home at Easter Road. On 28 March 1929 a fire caused considerable damage to the Pavilion at Parkhead. As the Grant Stand was being demolished at the same time, Celtic were forced to play their final matches away from Parkhead, and on 13 April of that year Hibs played Celtic at Easter Road, winning 4–1. This is one of Hibs biggest 'away' wins for this fixture to this day.

In front of 10,000 fans the Hibees that day were: Harris, Wilkinson, Urquhart, Finlay, Dick, Gilfeather, Frew, Brown, McColl, Halligan and Bradley. Brown, Gilfeather and McColl scored for Hibs, along with an own goal.

HE'S THE GAFFER

Dan McMichael	1900–3
Phil Kelso	1903–4
Dan McMichael	1904–19
Davy Gordon	1919–21
Alex Maley	1921–25
Bobby Templeton	1925–36
Willie McCartney	1936–48
Hugh Shaw	1948–61
Walter Galbraith	1961–4
Jock Stein	1964–5
Bob Shankley	1965–9
Willie Mcfarlane	1969–70
Dave Ewing	1970–71
Eddie Turnbull	1971–80
Willie Ormond	1980
Bertie Auld	1980–2
Pat Stanton	1982–4
John Blackley	1984–6
Alex Miller	1986–96
Jim Duffy	1996–8
Alex McLeish	1998–2001
Franck Sauzée	2001–2
Bobby Williamson	2002–4
Tony Mowbray	2004–6
John Collins	2006–7
Mixu Paatelainen	2008–9
John Hughes	2009–10
Colin Calderwood	2010–11
Pat Fenlon	2011–

Prior to 1900, the Hibs team was selected by a committee.

HE'S THE SHORT-TERM GAFFER

Hibs have had a number of stop-gap/caretaker managers between permanently appointed managers:

Billy Brown
Alistair Stevenson and Gareth Evans
Mark Proctor and John Park
Mark Venus
Gerry McCabe and Jim Clark
Donald Park
Billy McNeill
Jocky Scott

Jocky Scott had the longest spell as caretaker, taking over from Alex Miller for 13 games in late 1996 before he was replaced by Jim Duffy.

Tommy Craig was also caretaker boss for a total of 8 games, spread over 21 years. He originally stood in for John Blackley after he resigned in 1986 and before Alex Miller was appointed to replace him. He returned to Easter Road in 2006 as assistant manager to John Collins, and was part of the backroom team that lifted the CIS Cup in 2007. When Collins resigned later that year he became caretaker manager once more. He left when Mixu Paatelainen was appointed as full-time manager. Craig didn't enjoy much luck as caretaker manager – Hibs lost 6 of the 8 games he was in charge, and didn't record a single victory.

JUST NOT CRICKET

Andy Goram was one of the most recent examples of sportsmen who were able to compete in cricket and football to international standard, as the demands of modern sport means this becomes uncommon. Indeed, such was the burden of his full-time professional football career, Goram made just 4 appearances for Scotland at cricket. He was a right-arm medium-pacer and a batsman of reasonable standard, making a high score of 32 and best bowling figures of 2-42. He represented Scotland against the touring Australians in 1989, which led to him being fined as he did not have the permission of Hibs to play.

JUST NOT, ERM, BASKETBALL

Ólafur 'Ole' Gottskálksson was an Icelandic goalkeeper who arrived at Hibs with a big reputation during the summer of 1997 as Jim Duffy made sweeping changes around the club to try to move it forward.

Ole, however, was soon finding himself under siege in goal as Hibs struggled badly against relegation and confidence sank, culminating in Ole losing his place in the side to Chris Reid and then Bryan Gunn, who arrived from Norwich City.

Gottskálksson regained his place the following season, after Gunn suffered a career-ending injury during the summer break, and ended up with a First Division winners medal for his efforts. He lost his place the following season to Nick Colgan, and left for Brentford soon afterwards.

He represented Iceland twice while at Hibs for a grand total of 9 caps. He was a dual international too, having represented Iceland at basketball in his younger years. His career ended in 2005 at Torquay, when he absconded when he was selected for a random drugs test and he was banned.

FAMOUS SONS

Jimmy McGhee was an exceptional half-back for Hibernian in the latter part of the nineteenth century, captaining Hibs to Scottish Cup victory in 1887, and the year before becoming one of the first Hibs players to be capped by Scotland. He left Hibs to play for St Bernards, before moving on to Celtic. After retiring he was to become manager of Hearts, before emigrating to the USA.

His family moved with him, and one of his sons showed a particular aptitude for football just like his dad. Bart was to become a full international, just as his dad had been, but he played for his adopted country. Indeed, his 3 caps all came at the first World Cup in 1930, where he contributed two goals including the first goal scored by the USA in World Cup history. In 1986 he was inducted into the United States soccer hall of fame posthumously, having died in 1979.

FAMOUS DAUGHTERS

Gerry Baker was an exceptional striker for Hibs who replaced his brother Joe when he left for Torino. Gerry was an exciting player in his own right, and once scored 10 goals in a single cup tie for St Mirren and indeed won a Scottish Cup winner's medal with them in 1959.

Gerry was American by birth, but his daughters Karen and Lorraine were born in England and both turned out to be excellent athletes. Lorraine was good enough to compete in two Olympics in 1988 and 1996, finishing fifth in the 800m in Seoul, South Korea.

. . . AND FAMOUS GRANDSONS

Roy Erskine was centre-half who signed for Hibs in 1952 – slap bang in the middle of the most successful team in the club's history. In common with many players, he simply was unable to break into the championship-winning sides and he left in 1954 to go to Peebles Rovers, before going on to to play league football with Stirling Albion and Cowdenbeath for the rest of the decade.

His grandsons Andy Murray and Jamie Murray are professional tennis players, and Hibs fans. Andy is the top male British tennis player having reached four grand slam finals and has won 22 career titles to date including a gold medal at London 2012.

. . . AND FAMOUS SONS AND GRANDSONS

In 1932, a young Scotsman travelled all the way over from New Zealand to play for Hibs. Andrew Leslie was a sriker and played 10 games for the club, scoring 4 goals, including one on his debut in a Scottish Cup home defeat against Dundee United. This was a wretched season for Hibernian as they failed to bounce straight back up to the First Division and there was a high turnover of players, Leslie moving on to Bo'ness before returning to New Zealand.

He had originally gone to New Zealand in 1927 and is said to have been picked twice at the age of 14 to play for Scotland's schoolboys against England as a centre-half. In New Zealand he moved to the centre forward position where his 5ft 11in and 12st 11lb frame, coupled with a fair turn of speed, a fine shot and good ability with his head, ideally suited him for the role.

He made four appearances for the New Zealand national team, one against Australia in 1936 and three against England Amateurs in 1937. He died in 1964.

Andrew's son, also Andrew or 'Andy' as he was better known was also a talented footballer although of the rugby version, and was an All Black who captained the side in all of the 34 matches he played for the side including all 10 Tests. A combative number 8, he played against the country of his father's birth in 1975 before he retired from international rugby in 1976.

Andrew junior had two sons who were both excellent rugby players – John who was a centre and Martin who was a back row forward. They both represented Scotland as so called 'kilted kiwis' and qualified through their grandfather who had played for Hibs all those years ago. Both were to go on to represent Scotland in the World Cup and play against New Zealand.

FATHER AND SON

Several father and son pairings have represented Hibs over the years, some of them include:

Murdo MacLeod and Murdo MacLeod Junior
Jock Paterson and Craig Paterson
Joe McBride and Joe McBride Junior
Allan McGraw and Mark McGraw

In addition another couple of former players had fathers that had signed for Hibs but didn't actually play any games:

Jimmy Kane and Paul Kane
Lew Goram and Andy Goram

Then there are the Marshalls – Gordon Senior played for Hibs, and Gordon Junior was a goalkeeping coach in the 2000s. Although Gordon Junior never actually played for Hibs, he did sit on the bench as an unused substitute on a few occasions.

RECORD SALE

Hibernian's record transfer received is £4.4 million from Celtic for Scott Brown in May 2007. He had been with Hibs from his youth days and made his first-team debut at 17 going on to score 20 goals in 134 senior appearances. He also managed to rack up 37 yellow cards and 2 red cards in his time with the Hibees.

RECORD BUY

Hibernian's record incoming transfer was Ecuadorian full-back Ulises De La Cruz, who arrived in a complicated £750,000 deal from LDU Quito, but he had been playing for Barcelona of Ecuador at the time. After a season at Hibs scoring 2 goals in 39 appearances he moved on to Aston Villa after starring for Ecuador in the 2002 World Cup for £2 million. During his time at Hibs he scored one of the quickest ever derby goals beating Antti Niemi after 37 seconds of the October 2001 Edinburgh clash. Ulises, described as the Ecuadorian Roberto Carlos, went on to win 99 caps for his country scoring 6 goals and enjoying a long career in England with Aston Villa before moving on to Reading and Birmingham City. After his contract expired with Birmingham he returned to his previous club, LDU Quito. Away from football he set up a charity, Friends of FundeCruz which funds projects in his home town.

CHAMPIONS I – 1893/94

This was the year when Hibernian won a national league for the first time in their history, yet failed to gain promotion. The years since the club had won the Scottish Cup in 1887 had been difficult, with Celtic recruiting widely from Hibs' ranks, and they also had internal problems that led to them losing their ground and withdrawing from football for a period – a dreadful fate to befall the club so soon after being the first eastern side to win the Scottish Cup.

Like a phoenix rising from the ashes, Hibs got their affairs in order, and the newly developing Scottish League was next on the agenda. In 1893, Hibs were founder members of the Second Division but were far too good for most of the other sides, and won the league scoring goals at an incredible average of over 4 a game. These were the days before automatic promotion, though, and teams were selected for promotion by the governing body. Despite beating Clyde at home and away, Hibs were denied entry to the top level, and Clyde were voted into the First Division instead.

Hibs clinched the title with their final game of the season, when they thrashed Port Glasgow Athletic 10–1 at Easter Road to move clear of Cowlairs.

Scottish League Division Two

	P	W	D	L	F	A	Pts
Hibernian	18	13	3	2	83	29	29
Cowlairs	18	13	1	4	72	32	27
Clyde	18	11	2	5	51	36	24
Motherwell	18	11	1	6	61	46	23
Partick Thistle	18	10	0	8	56	58	20
Port Glasgow Athletic	18	9	2	7	52	52	13
Abercorn	18	5	2	11	42	59	12
Morton	18	4	1	13	36	62	9
Northern	18	3	3	12	29	66	9
Thistle	18	2	3	13	31	72	7

Results

19 Aug	A	Thistle	2–1 W
26 Aug	H	Morton	9–2 W
9 Sep	A	Clyde	4–0 W
16 Sep	H	Abercorn	7–2 W
30 Sep	A	Northern	2–2 D
7 Oct	H	Cowlairs	4–3 L
21 Oct	A	Port Glasgow Athletic	3–3 D
4 Nov	H	Thistle	4–0 W
25 Nov	H	Motherwell	8–2 W
2 Dec	A	Morton	1–0 W
3 Feb	H	Partick Thistle	6–1 W
3 Mar	A	Abercorn	3–3 D
10 Mar	H	Clyde	4–3 W
17 Mar	A	Cowlairs	3–2 W

31 Mar	A	Partick Thistle	7–1 W
7 Apr	H	Northern	6–0 W
14 Apr	A	Motherwell	2–1 L
19 May	H	Port Glasgow Athletic	10–1 W

Appearances

Allan Martin	16
John Kennedy	16
James McGeachan	15
Pat Murray	15
William Smith	15
Joseph Murphy	14
Alex Howie	14
Barney Breslin	14
Hugh Rooney	12
Willie Donnelly	10
Tom McFarlane	9
Patrick Cowan	7
John Quigley	6
James Murphy	3
Charles Amos	2
Trialists	2
John Mitchell	1
Clark	1
Adam Hutchison	1
P. Doyle	1
Goldie	1
Jo Murphy	1
John Scott	1

Goalscorers

Allan Martin	10
Alex Howie	10
William Smith	6
Joseph Murphy	5
Pat Murray	3

John Kennedy	3
Charlie Amos	3
James McGeachan	1
Untraced	43 goals

QUICKEST GOALS

Anthony Stokes holds the distinction of scoring the fastest ever SPL goal for Hibs, notching after just 12.4 seconds against Rangers on 27 December 2009 at Easter Road. Despite the flying start, Hibs crashed 4–1.

UNBEATEN RUNS

The longest Hibernian have ever gone without defeat is 24 games, in wartime league and cup games. After beating Celtic at Easter Road in the Scottish Southern League Cup Group B of 1941/42 on 28 March, Hibs negotiated games in the Scottish Southern League and Summer Cup and the first 14 games of the following season's Southern League before finally losing heavily to Clyde 7–2 in November 1942.

They were unbeaten in wartime league games at home between November 1941 and November 1943 – a total of 32 games.

From October 1949 onwards Hibernian were unbeaten for 15 games in a row on the road in all competitions, and from August 1964 Hibs won 9 games in a row away from home.

At home, beginning from 29 December 1945, Hibernian won 16 games in a row at Easter Road, before losing out to Hearts in September 1946.

SCOTTISH FOOTBALL LEAGUE RECORDS

Hibs share the highest home score – when they beat Hamilton Academical on 6 November 1965 11–1. Just 6,319 were present to see Wilson, Simpson, Davis, Stanton, McNamee, Baxter, Hogg, Cormack, Scott, O'Rourke and Stevenson take the field. Goalscorers were Davis, Hogg, Cormack, Scott (2), O'Rourke (2) and Stevenson (3).

Hibs have the highest away score in the top league too – when they won 11–1 at Airdrie on 24 October 1959. The team that day was Wilson, Grant, McClelland, Young, Plenderleith, Baxter, MacLeod, Johnstone, Baker, Preston and Ormond. In front of 7,000 fans, McLelland, McLeod (2), Baker (3), Preston (4) and Ormond were the goalscorers.

Hibs were also involved in the highest scoring draw when they drew 6–6 with Motherwell in May 2010. They had been ahead 6–2 before being clawed back and although goalkeeper Graeme Smith had managed to save a penalty to keep Hibernian ahead 6–5, Motherwell equalised in the dying minutes. The team in front of a crowd of 6,241 was: Smith, Thicot, Hanlon, Hogg, Murray, Wotherspoon, Rankin, Miller, Nish, Riordan (McBride), Stokes (Benjelloun). Colin Nish scored a hat-trick, Derek Riordan scored and Anthony Stokes chipped in with a double.

THEY DIED WITH THEIR BOOTS ON

Jimmy Main was an outstanding right-back who signed for Hibs from Motherwell in 1904 while still in his teens. Main was to establish himself in the Hibs team over the next five years, and his excellent play and form drew attention from firstly the Scottish League, who capped him in 1908, and then the full international team in 1909 when he was capped for Scotland in the annual fixture against Ireland.

Main was to suffer the cruellest of fates in Hibs colours. On Christmas Day 1909, in a match played at Firhill against Partick Thistle on an icy pitch, he was kicked in the stomach accidentally by a Partick Thistle player and suffered a ruptured spleen. After the match, Main had returned home but was admitted to the Edinburgh Royal Infirmary when the magnitude of his injuries was recognised. At first an emergency operation appeared to have positive results but additional treatment was unsuccessful and Main died from his injuries on 29 December.

Jimmy had been born in West Calder in 1886, and made his debut against Dundee in September 1904 at Dens Park. He was to go on to make 150 appearances for Hibs, scoring 4 goals and winning 1 Scotland Cap, and 1 Scottish League cap. He was just 23 when he died.

A mere six years later, Hibs were to lose another player to an untimely death when centre forward Jimmy Hendren died. Born in Annbank to Irish ancestry in about 1887, Hendren was a miner by trade. He had worked in the Ayrshire mines and played for Kilmarnock before emigrating to America. He later returned to Scotland, to Fife, where he played football for Cowdenbeath and worked in the mines. It was from Cowdenbeath he was spotted and signed for Hibs in 1911. A strong, quick striker he was well established at Hibs, and played in the 1914 side that lost the Scottish Cup final.

Sadly, he died suddenly in June 1919 in his late twenties, leaving behind a widow and two young children. Hibs requested permission from the wartime authorities to play a benefit match but this was refused, and instead a donation was made from their funds. He had been top scorer in his 3 full seasons at Hibernian, scoring 56 goals in 135 appearances, from his debut against Queen's Park in October 1911 until his final appearance, also against Queen's Park, in April 1915. He scored a hat-trick on his final appearance. In future years, Jimmy Hendren's great nephew – Pat Stanton – was to make a name for himself at Hibs.

YOUNGEST SIDE

In 2007, Hibs fielded a side against Aberdeen at Pittodrie with an average age of just 20 years 355 days. Although their inexperience told, and they finished with just 9 men, they managed a creditable 2–2 draw. Damon Gray, who had made his debut the previous week in the Scottish Cup semi-final against Dunfermline at Hampden opened his Hibs goalscoring account.

This beat the previous record set in 1983 when Hibernian had played a very young and inexperienced side against Airdrie in a meaningless League Cup sectional tie. Mickey Weir and Callum Milne made their debuts in a team including teenagers Robin Rae, Paul Kane, Gordon Hunter and Kevin McKee. Hibs won 3–1.

UNLUCKIEST INTERNATIONAL

Tommy Bogan was one of the original 'McCartney Babes' who joined Hibs in 1943. He made his debut against Falkirk in October, scoring, and went on to be a prolific scorer; he notched 42 goals in just 66 games in wartime competitions. His form caught the eye of the Scotland selectors who named him in the side for an international fixture against England in 1945. However, he twisted his knee in the first minute, was substituted and would never gain a full cap for Scotland. He left Hibs early the following year for Celtic, but wasn't to enjoy the same fortune, moving on to Manchester United, Aberdeen and Southampton, again with little success. He was to rue leaving Hibs just as they became the dominant force in Scottish football.

After football Bogan worked in the newspaper industry, and was actually married to Sir Matt Busby's niece.

CHAMPIONS II – 1894/95

Hibs started the season in Division Two, and were as dominant as they were the previous campaign when they'd won the league but not been elected up. This time their promotion could not be avoided and the clubs voted for Hibs to be promoted to Division One. Hibs clinched the title on 4 May when they beat Renton 9–1, the only team that could catch them by that point.

Scottish League Division Two

	P	W	D	L	F	A	Pts
Hibernian	18	14	2	2	92	28	30
Motherwell	18	10	2	6	56	39	22
Port Glasgow Athletic	18	8	4	6	62	56	20
Renton *	17	10	0	7	46	44	20
Morton	18	9	1	8	59	63	19
Airdrie	18	8	2	8	68	45	18
Abercorn	18	7	4	7	51	65	18
Partick Thistle	18	7	3	8	50	62	17
Dundee Wanderers *	17	3	1	13	44	86	9
Cowlairs	18	2	3	13	37	77	7

*Renton did not turn up for their fixture at Dundee Wanderers, hence only 17 games were played by both clubs. Dundee were awarded both points for the game.

18 Aug	H	Partick Thistle	5–1 W
1 Sep	A	Abercorn	5–1 W
8 Sep	H	Dundee Wanderers	8–2 W
15 Sep	H	Airdrieonians	6–1 W
6 Oct	A	Motherwell	2–0 L
13 Oct	A	Morton	7–1 W
20 Oct	H	Morton	6–3 W
3 Nov	H	Abercorn	4–2 W
10 Nov	A	Dundee Wanderers	6–0 W
17 Nov	A	Renton	3–2 L

22 Dec	H	Cowlairs	8–2 W
2 Feb	H	Motherwell	5–0 W
9 Mar	A	Port Glasgow Athletic	2–2 D
16 Mar	A	Cowlairs	8–2 W
6 Apr	H	Port Glasgow Athletic	3–3 D
13 Apr	A	Partick Thistle	4–0 W
4 May	H	Renton	9–1 W
25 May	A	Airdrieonians	4–2 W

Appearances

Pat Murray	16
Allan Martin	16
Joseph Murphy	15
John Kennedy	15
Tom McFarlane	14
Barney Breslin	14
Robert Neill	14
Willie Donnelly	11
William Smith	11
Charlie Amos	6
Hugh Rooney	5
James McGeachan	5
Alex Howie	5
Michael Murray	5
Tom Robertson	4
James McGinn	4
Arthur Brady	3
Paddy Smith	2
John Scott	1
Barnes	1
Rourke	1
Devlin	1

Goals

Allan Martin	17
William Smith	8
Pat Murray	7

John Kennedy	5
Robert Neill	4
Alex Howie	4
Joseph Murphy	3
Michael Murray	3
James McGeachan	2
Arthur Brady	2
Barnes	1
Untraced	39

THE FASTEST HIBBY

Some will claim that Ivan Sproule is the fastest they have ever seen, others will say it's Arthur Duncan. This quandary is easy to solve, though – the fastest ever Hibby was George McNeil from Tranent.

George played but a single game for Hibs, against St Johnstone in December 1965, moving on to Morton and then Stirling Albion before retiring from football at the age of 22 to concentrate on a full-time professional athletics career. It was a different era back then, and because of the professional sporting contracts that George had in football, it debarred him from pursuing an amateur athletics career – and also from competing in major championships including the Olympics.

George won a string of titles and awards in a glittering career including the 100th Powderhall New Year Sprint, and the 100th edition of the Stawell Gift in Australia. He was also the world professional sprint champion of 1972. He set a world record of 11.14 seconds for the 120 yards at Meadowbank in August 1970.

He was inducted into the Scottish Sports Hall of Fame in 2003, alongside fellow Hibernian footballer Gordon Smith.

THEY SAID IT

'The trouble with you son is that your brains are all in your head.'

Eddie Turnbull to Alan Gordon

DOUBLE CHAMPION

Alan Sneddon was a defender who joined Hibs from Celtic in January 1981 and was to go on to be a mainstay of the team over the next decade. He had been a regular at Celtic, impressing against Real Madrid in the quarter-finals of the European Cup. He was also a Scottish under-21 international. With Hibernian he played in the 1985 Skol Cup losing team, but was in the squad when they won the Skol Cup in 1991.

However, his only winner's medal with Hibs came within a few months of joining as Hibernian celebrated winning the Scottish First Division in 1981. Sneddon had played enough games to receive a medal, but as it turned out, he had also played enough games in the Scottish Premier League to win a medal too – as Celtic won their division as well.

SHORTEST CAREER

Ian Hendry was reputed to have the shortest career ever, after he broke his leg just 20 seconds into his debut against Berwick Rangers in January 1981. In fact he returned to fitness and played a second time against Partick Thistle in March 1982. He left for Nuneaton Borough, before going on to play for Gloucester City, Cambridge United, Worcester City and Stafford Rangers.

Many players have played for Hibs just a single time, and indeed some subs have come on with a short amount of time to go. Probably the shortest of those was John Kane, who appeared as an 89th minute substitute against Livingston in 2003. He never played another game for Hibernian, subsequently playing for Glenafton Athletic, and with Stranraer.

BOGEY TEAMS

Hibs only ever met Arthurlie twice, losing both times. The two sides clashed in the Scottish Cup in 1882 and in the first leg Hibernian lost 4–3 at home. A replay was ordered, and the sides met at Arthurlie three weeks later. Arthurlie won this time 6–0 and the sides never met again. Arthurlie now play in the West Super League Premier Division.

Rugby Park, Kilmarnock, has not been a happy hunting ground for Hibs in recent times, but it's nothing compared to the 19-plus-year drought further back in time. After beating Kilmarnock in December 1957, Hibernian failed to record a victory in Ayrshire until February 1977 – a run of 23 games and nearly 20 years. The run included a spell of 14 straight losses.

Hibernian also had a torrid time against Aberdeen at home from 1983 for the following 7 years, failing to win for 13 games. Hibs eventually won in March 1990 when Paul Wright scored the winner in a 3–2 victory. Alan Sneddon was the only player who played in both the 1983 and 1990 games.

The biggest bogeys of the lot, though, are unsurprisingly the Old Firm duo of Rangers and Celtic. If you thought that the results in recent years have been hard to take, spare a thought for Hibs fans in the early part of the twentieth century. After winning at both Ibrox and Parkhead in the championship winning season of 1902/03, Hibernian failed to record a league win against either side in Glasgow for another 21 years, before finally beating Rangers 2–1 in 1924 and Celtic 3–2 in 1927. These runs constituted an eye-watering run of 25 games at Pakhead and 20 games at Ibrox without a win. Bizarrely both those wins in 1902/03 were record away victories that have been matched since, but haven't been broken to this day.

In recent times Hibernian went from 1995 to 2005 without winning in Glasgow, between a 1–0 Darren Jackson-inspired victory at Ibrox on 23 September 1995, and a 30 April 2005 3–1 win at Parkhead, with O'Connor, Brown and Sproule scoring.

GLAD TO SEE YOU

Hibs have never lost a game at Easter Road against Alloa Athletic. Since their first meeting in 1923, they have met 14 times, with Hibs winning 12 of the meetings, and drawing the other 2. Hibs have racked up an impressive 41 goals in that time, while conceding just 7.

On the road, Hibs had an outstanding record at Hamilton. After losing 3–1 in March 1942 in the Southern League Cup, Hibs went undefeated until losing in September 2009 – a run of 20 games. The luck appears to have deserted Hibs, as they have now lost on three of their last four visits to Hamilton.

LEGENDS – ARTHUR DUNCAN

In December 1969, Hibernian accepted an offer for their teenage sensation Peter Marinello from Arsenal, and manager Willie Macfarlane moved quickly to secure the services of Arthur Duncan with the proceeds. Duncan was to go on to play 626 games for Hibernian, scoring over 100 goals.

He was born in Hamilton in 1947, and moved to Partick Thistle from Falkirk High. He had racked up over 100 appearances at Thistle before joining Hibs. In his debut against Celtic he scored, but the game ended in a 2–1 defeat at Easter Road.

His speed was a feature of his play and he became a crucial part of Turnbull's Tornadoes, not only scoring himself but supplying the crosses for Jimmy O'Rourke and Alan Gordon to score. At the team's pinnacle in 1972/73, Duncan scored 22 goals – he was to break 10 goals for the season on 5 occasions.

He played in the Hibs team which made the Scottish Cup final in 1979, taking Rangers to three games (in the days before penalty shoot-outs), before losing 3–2. Arthur had the unfortunate distinction of scoring Rangers' winner with an unlucky own goal.

He was a pretty handy goalkeeper too, having to deputise between the sticks after injury to Jim McArthur in the days before substitute goalkeepers. Later in his career he moved to left-back, and performed admirably there.

Duncan made his final competitive appearance for Hibs in April 1984 in a 1–0 victory over Dundee United, before breaking his collarbone the following week in an east of Scotland game against Meadowbank Thistle. He was freed at the end of the season and moved on to Meadowbank where he played for a couple of more seasons late into his thirties. After retiring he became the Meadowbank physio, before becoming a chiropodist. He retired to Australia.

With Hibs, only Gordon Smith played more often and Duncan won League Cup honours in 1972, along with the Drybrough Cup in 1972 and 1973. He won 6 Scotland caps and is an original inductee into the Hibs Hall of Fame.

EASTER ROAD IN EUROPE

Hibs aren't the only team to have played at Easter Road in Europe – the ground was borrowed by Raith Rovers for their second round UEFA Cup game in 1995. Raith lost the home leg 2–0, losing 4–1 on aggregate.

INTERNATIONALS AT EASTER ROAD

Since Easter Road was renovated in 1995, the ground has been used by Scotland for a series of friendlies. These have been:

22 April 1998, Scotland 1–1 Finland
Future Hibs manager Colin Calderwood started for Scotland, and former Hibs striker Darren Jackson also featured. Another future Hibee, Jonatan Johansson, scored for Finland in this warm up game for the 1998 World Cup.

15 October 2002, Scotland 3–1 Canada
Paul Fenwick captained Canada on his home ground, but was unable to prevent them going down to a Stevie Crawford-inspired Scotland side, the former Hibs striker scoring two of the goals. Hibs' young midfielder Ian Murray came off the bench to win the first of his six Scotland caps.

30 May 2004, Scotland 4–1 Trinidad & Tobago
Scotland eased past a Trinidad side without many of its star players. Hibs defender Gary Caldwell scored for Scotland, before being subbed for his brother Steven.

17 November 2004, Scotland 1–4 Sweden
Scotland lost for the first time at Easter Road, in a game in which featured Ian Murray as well as past Hibs strikers Stevie Crawford and Kenny Miller.

15 August 2012, Scotland 3–1 Australia
Craig Levein's side recorded a fine victory against a strong Australian team. Jordan Rhodes and Ross McCormack scored either side of a Jason Davidson own goal.

One other international has been played at Easter Road, and that was the game between Ghana and South Korea in the run-up to the 2006 World Cup. Ghana won 3–1, Michael Essien notching one of the goals.

RUGBY AT EASTER ROAD

Easter Road was also the home ground of the Edinburgh professional rugby union team for a season, back in 1998/99, when the team played their Heineken Cup matches at the football ground. Despite further discussions, no more rugby matches have been played at the ground since.

SEMI-FINALS AT EASTER ROAD

In the Scottish Cup, there have been several semi-finals played at Easter Road, although there's only been one in the last 50 years. These are:

1925 Dundee 2–0 Hamilton (replay, first game had taken place at Tynecastle)

1937 Aberdeen 2–0 Morton

1949 Clyde 2–2 Dundee AET (the replay was played at Hampden this time)

1952 Dundee 2–0 Third Lanark

1955 Aberdeen 0–1 Clyde (after 2–2 draw)

1956 Hearts 3–1 Raith Rovers (after 0–0 draw)

1997 Kilmarnock 1–0 Dundee United (after 0–0 draw)

In the League Cup, there have been more games, mainly involving Hearts, when they dominated the competition in the late 1950s and early '60s.

1947 Aberdeen 6–2 Hearts

1954 Hearts 4–1 Airdrie

1958 Hearts 3–0 Kilmarnock

1959 Hearts 9–3 Cowdenbeath

1961 Hearts 2–1 Stirling Albion AET

1962 Hearts 4–0 St Johnstone

1996 Hearts 3–1 Dundee

1998 St Johnstone 3–0 Hearts

2004 Dundee 0–1 Livingston

2005 Hearts 2–3 Motherwell AET

2006 Dunfermline 1–0 Livingston

CONCERTS

The Easter Road stadium has excellent facilities especially now that the redevelopment is complete with the opening of the East Stand in 2010. In June 2005 it also hosted its first ever concert when Elton John played there, with the ever-popular Glaswegian singer Lulu as support. Despite the success of the event, there have been no further concerts to date.

GROUND DEVELOPMENT

The face of Easter Road has changed greatly in the last 20 years, from a primarily standing venue into the superb all-seater stadium that it is today. This work was done in several phases dating back to 1995. The last component was the East Stand which was knocked down and rebuilt in 2010, to complement the Main Stand which had been rebuilt in 2001. Prior to this the two ends behind the goals – the North and South Stands – had been upgraded in 1995. These developments took place on the back of the Taylor Report which had been commissioned after the dreadful events at Hillsborough when 96 Liverpool fans lost their lives.

In the period up until 1995, benches had been installed into Easter Road to comply with legislation but this was only a short-term measure and the ground was completely rebuilt under the stewardship of Sir Tom Farmer.

Prior to this, Easter Road had seen the old Main Stand constructed in 1924, but was largely a terraced ground from then until the 1960s when a roof was added over the North Stand and benches installed. This was affectionately called the Cowshed. The vast terraces on the east side of the ground were reduced in size and a roof was added in 1985 reducing the capacity down from 65,000 to 27,000. Presently the capacity of the ground is 20,421 which makes it the fifth biggest football stadium in Scotland after Parkhead, Hampden, Ibrox and Pittodrie.

The Easter Road pitch used to be famous for its considerable slope which ran from the South End to the North End of the ground. This was finally levelled out in 2000, in preparation for the West Stand being built the following season. The final game on the slope was against Aberdeen in April 2000, and Hibs ran out 1–0 winners. Kenny Miller scored the only goal of the game.

The pitch at the stadium has dimensions of 105m x 68m, which make it a full international size pitch.

CHAMPIONS III – 1902/03

This was a landmark season for Hibernian as they won their first national top league title. Dundee had been the early pacesetters, while Hibs had faltered against Third Lanark and dropped points against Hearts and Celtic. However, a victory over Rangers at Easter Road set them up nicely for their first meeting with Dundee and Hibs duly responded by notching a victory in this game as well. Hibernian thereafter romped to the title with 11 wins and 3 draws in their final 14 games. There were thumping wins at Rangers and Dundee by three clear goals, and they went one better at Parkhead. David Reid finished the season as top scorer with a prolific 15 goals from 16 games.

It had been a glorious year for Hibs, and their manager Dan McMichael, as they had clinched the Scottish Cup just eight months earlier. It was to be another 45 years before they added another league title.

Scottish League Division One

	P	W	D	L	F	A	Pts
Hibernian	22	16	5	1	48	18	37
Dundee	22	13	5	4	31	12	31
Rangers	22	12	5	5	56	30	29
Hearts	22	11	6	5	46	27	28
Celtic	22	8	10	4	36	30	26
St Mirren	22	7	8	7	39	40	22
Third Lanark	22	8	5	9	34	27	21
Partick Thistle	22	6	7	9	34	50	19
Kilmarnock	22	6	4	12	24	43	16
Queen's Park	22	5	5	12	33	48	15
Port Glasgow Athletic	22	3	5	14	26	49	11
Morton	22	2	5	15	22	55	9

16 Aug	H	Celtic	1–1 D
23 Aug	A	Port Glasgow Athletic	1–0 W
30 Aug	H	Queen's Park	3–2 W
6 Sep	A	Kilmarnock	4–1 W
13 Sep	H	Hearts	0–0 D
15 Sep	H	Rangers	1–0 W
20 Sep	A	Third Lanark	1–0 L
27 Sep	H	Dundee	1–0 W
29 Sep	A	Rangers	5–2 W
4 Oct	H	St Mirren	4–3 W
11 Oct	A	Hearts	1–1 D
18 Oct	H	Morton	3–1 W
25 Oct	A	Dundee	3–0 W
1 Nov	H	Partick Thistle	2–2 D
8 Nov	A	Queen's Park	3–1 W
15 Nov	H	Kilmarnock	2–1 W
22 Nov	H	Third Lanark	1–0 W
29 Nov	A	St Mirren	1–1 D
6 Dec	A	Morton	1–0 W
20 Dec	A	Partick Thistle	2–0 W
2 Jan	A	Celtic	4–0 W
31 Jan	H	Port Glasgow Athletic	5–1 W

Appearances

Harry Rennie	22
Bobby Atherton	22
Patrick Callaghan	21
James Buchan	21
Alex Robertson	20
J. Stewart	19
Barney Breslin	19
Archie Gray	18
Billy McCartney	17
David Reid	16
James Hogg	15
James Harrower	11

Andrew McGeachan	10
Robert Glen	3
Tom Bone	3
Alex Logan	2
Johnny Divers	2
Hamilton Handling	1

Goals

David Reid	15
Patrick Callaghan	9
J. Stewart	9
Bobby Atherton	5
Billy McCartney	5
James Buchan	2
Archie Gray	2
Barney Breslin	1

ONE WILLIE MILLER?

Or not, as the case may be. Four players by this name have worn the Hibernian colours, the most recent one being the right-back who played in the Skol Cup-winning team of 1991. He played 287 games for Hibs, scoring 3 goals before moving on to Dundee when Hibernian were relegated in 1998.

One of his namesakes was the half-back who played in the 1923 and 1924 Scottish Cup finals, making 301 appearances for Hibs and scoring 32 goals.

The other two Willie Millers played a handful of games between them, one was a goalkeeper in the mid-1950s, and the other played at the turn of the century.

In addition, Hibs have had three John Campbells, two Willie Allans, two David Reids, two John Hughes and two Jimmy Harrowers.

However, the two pairs of namesakes that gave reporters the biggest headaches were the John Grants and the Jim Browns as they both played at the same time.

John Grant was an established defender, when Johnny Grant appeared in the team in 1963. They played together for a single season. Jim Brown was a veteran by the time he joined Hibs from Hearts in 1979, and the defender was joined by Jimmy Brown who had transferred in from Portsmouth in 1980. After playing in the same team for a short spell they both left the club in 1981, Jim for Dunfermline where his career would be ended by a John Pelosi challenge, and Jimmy for Worcester City.

MOST CHANGES

When Hibernian drew the 1914 Scottish Cup final against Celtic, the replay was ordered for the following Thursday. This created a minor problem as Hibs already had a league game scheduled for the Wednesday at home to Dumbarton. In a move that would probably earn them the wrath of modern-day administrators, Hibernian rested their entire side with the exception of the goalkeeper for the following day's game. Hibs drew the league game 1–1, and the side appeared fresh for the cup final replay the following day. However, it was not enough on this occasion and they fell to a 4–1 defeat with future Hibs striker Jimmy McColl scoring for Celtic.

GEORGE BURLEY AND ALAN HANSEN

So what could former Scotland manager George Burley and football pundit Alan Hansen possibly have in common in a Hibs context?

The answer is surprisingly simple – they have both scored for Hibs, two of the many players to have contributed an own goal to the Hibernian cause. Burley scored the winner while playing for Motherwell in 1989 in a 1–0 Hibs victory, while Partick Thistle's Hansen was on the target to give Hibs a share of the points in a fixture at Easter Road in January 1975.

RED CARDS IN THEIR FINAL GAMES

Grant Brebner arrived at Hibs initially on loan from Manchester United, and was Scotland under-21 captain. After his loan spell ended, he moved on to Reading before returning to Easter Road in autumn 1999. After a turbulent first couple of seasons he became a regular under Bobby Williamson. When Bobby Williamson left and Tony Mowbray took over Brebner didn't last long – just four games. Against Motherwell in the second game of the season, Brebner received his marching orders along with Colin Murdock. Despite this, Hibernian held on for a 2–1 victory but Brebner never played for the club again, moving on to Dundee United before heading over to play in the Australian A League.

Grant is not the only the player to be sent off on their final bow; long-serving Gordon Hunter also suffered this fate in an altogether more important game – the SPL play-off match with Airdrie. Hibs were at home in the first leg, and had managed to scrape an early lead before Gordon got himself sent off before half time. The good news is that Hibs held on for the 1–0 victory, before going on to record a 4–2 victory at Broadwood the following Thursday in a match that featured four penalties. Steve Cooper, who had scored the own goal to give Hibs the advantage had been presented with an opportunity from the penalty spot to give Airdrie an aggregate lead. He missed, Darren Jackson scored two penalties and Hibs were 4–1 up on the night before former Jambo Kenny Black gave Airdrie a late consolation from the spot. Gordon, who had famously scored the winner to end Hearts' unbeaten run of 22 games against Hibs, never played for Hibernian again and moved to Australia before finishing his career at a lower level.

RED CARDS ON THEIR DEBUT

By the time that Hibs had made the Scottish Cup final in 2012, their on-loan captain James McPake had already been winning over the Hibs fans with a string of stirring performances after arriving from Coventry in January. However, he didn't have the most auspicious of starts – he was sent off on his debut at Ibrox as Hibs crashed to a 4–0 defeat.

SENT OFF ON DEBUT
AND FINAL APPEARANCE

Dermot McCaffrey was a prospect that many at Hibs had high hopes for. Northern Irish by birth, he arrived at the club from Dungannon Swifts and was a regular in the Northern Ireland under-21 side. He made his one and only appearance for Hibs in a league game at Pittodrie in 2007. Unfortunately he marked his appearance with a red card when he was sent off for a second bookable offence. He later spent some time on loan at Queen of the South and Livingston, and also played for Falkirk before heading back to Northern Ireland to play for Dungannon Swifts and Derry City.

HOW MANY DO YOU THINK HE'LL HAVE?

In 2005, Hibernian played Rangers at Ibrox and fielded a 4-5-1 formation. Scottish International Garry O'Connor was the lone striker, and with limited service he struggled to make an impact.

Midway through the second half the manager Tony Mowbray made a substitution – removing O'Connor and replacing him with Northern Irishman Ivan Sproule who had joined the club earlier that year from Northern Irish side Institute. Although he had scored in a win at Parkhead, he had made a limited impact up to this point, as he found his feet in Scottish football as a professional having only been part-time in Northern Ireland.

O'Connor was raging when he left the field, 'Why am I being subbed?' Mowbray replied, 'You've not had a shot on goal all day.' This did little to calm the agitated O'Connor who fired back with, 'and how many do you think he's going to f***ing have?'

Sproule, in only his 11th appearance in a Hibs jersey, all bar one of which had been from the substitutes' bench, proceeded to make the most of the 22 minutes he was given on the pitch and scored possibly the most incredible hat-trick ever produced by a visiting player at Ibrox.

The 3–0 result was all the more remarkable in that it was Hibernian's first win at Ibrox in nearly 10 years and equalled their biggest win ever at Rangers which had come 103 years earlier.

After the game, Mowbray was able to make light of O'Connor's ire, saying, 'Garry asked why he was being taken off and I told him it was because he hadn't had a shot at goal. He asked me how many I thought Ivan would have and afterwards I was able to tell him "at least three".'

Later on that same season, Hibs were to repeat the scoreline in another win, this time in the Scottish Cup. All the more pleasing was that the Rangers manager for these games was Alex McLeish who had left Hibernian in acrimonious circumstances a couple of years earlier. He left his post as Rangers manager at the end of the season.

PENALTY KING

The undisputed penalty king at Easter Road was Eddie Turnbull who scored an incredible 53 during his Easter Road career out of his total of 202 goals. In 1952/53 he scored 9 penalties in a season, including a run of 4 in 5 games. He also scored a hat-trick of penalties in a league game against Celtic.

Joe Davis managed to score 11 penalties in a season twice, consecutively in 1966/67 and 1967/68. In all he scored 39 penalties in his five years at Hibs, after joining from Third Lanark in 1964.

CAPPED AT 82

Eddie Turnbull, the legendary Hibs player and manager has an unusual distinction in being one of the oldest players ever to be capped for his country. Turnbull played 10 games for Scotland between 1948 and 1958, but at that time players only received a cap if they played against one of the home nations. This rule was relaxed in the mid-1970s and from this point on all players received a cap regardless of opposition. Gary Imlach, the broadcaster, had brought this anomaly to wider attention, in attempt to win a retrospective cap for his father Stewart who had played alongside Eddie in the 1958 World Cup. The SFA relented and all affected players received a cap. Eddie received his cap, and was introduced to the crowd at Hampden in a game against Switzerland in 2006. Other Hibs players who received the retrospective caps were Alex Cropley, Des Bremner, Jim Scott, Neil Martin, Erich Schaedler and Willie Hamilton.

THE SCOTTISH CUP

Since Hibernian won the Scottish Cup in 1902 they have played in the competition on 98 occasions. The cup was suspended during the First World War and the Second World War meaning the trophy was not played for on twelve occasions.

Hibs' record in the competition is legendary, leading to articles in the worldwide press about the long run without success. In that time Hibs have lost 9 finals, a heart rending 17 semi-finals, and 15 quarter-finals.

The full list of sides to have knocked Hibs out since their last victory in 1902 are as follows:

Aberdeen	13
Rangers	13
Celtic	12
Hearts	9
Dundee	5
Dundee United	5
Partick Thistle	5
Airdrieonians	4
Clyde	4
Motherwell	4
Raith Rovers	4
Dunfermline Athletic	3
East Fife	2
Kilmarnock	2
St Johnstone	2
Third Lanark	2
Arbroath	1
Armadale	1
Ayr United	1
Clydebank	1
Cowdenbeath	1
Edinburgh City	1
Hamilton Acadamical	1
Ross County	1
Stirling Albion	1

SUBSTITUTES

Substitutes have become an increasing influence in football since first being introduced in 1966. First it was one, then two, then three, then five and currently seven, of which three can come onto the field.

Hibernian's first selected substitute was Jimmy O'Rourke for a home game against Rangers in August 1966, although he wasn't called into action. The first one to actually come onto the field was Pat Quinn, who replaced Joe Davis in December in a 5–1 reverse against Clyde.

The first Hibs player to score after coming on from the bench in Scotland was John Murphy, who joined the fray in time to score the winner against Dunfermline (2–1) in April 1970. However, when Hibs were representing Toronto in the United States Soccer League in 1967, Colin Grant came on and scored a hat-trick against Boston. Boston were represented by Shamrock Rovers from the Republic of Ireland. Ivan Sproule of course, famously scored a hat-trick against Rangers at Ibrox after coming on as substitute for Garry O'Connor in 2005.

The player who has made the most appearances from the bench is Gareth Evans, who came on a total of 97 times during his playing career at the club, between 1991 and 2000. Gareth scored on his debut for Hibs against Dundee, after coming on as a sub – naturally. Abdessalam Benjelloun and Stephen Dobbie hold the record of substitute appearances in a season, both coming on 24 times – Stephen in 2003/04 and Benji in 2009/10.

CHAMPIONS IV – 1932/33

After relegation from the First Division in 1930/31, Hibernian's failure to bounce straight back at the first attempt had been as surprising as it was unwelcome, and the 1932/33 season saw the introduction of several new players in an attempt to freshen up the side for a serious promotion push. Three of these players – Robert Wallace, Rab Walls and Peter Flucker – were to bolster the forward line and scored 58 goals between them. The were aided by the last remaining player of the great team of the 1920s – Johnny Halligan.

Two significant runs were influential in their superiority – a run of 11 wins in 12 games in the autumn followed by a run of 12 wins in 13 from the winter into spring.

Bobby Templeton's Hibs clinched this title on 15 April after a win against Dumbarton, although promotion itself had been secured in previous weeks.

	P	W	D	L	F	A	Pts
Hibernian	34	25	4	5	80	29	54
Queen of the South	34	20	9	5	93	59	49
Dunfermline Athletic	34	20	7	7	89	44	47
Stenhousemuir	34	18	6	10	67	58	42
Albion Rovers	34	19	2	13	82	57	40
Raith Rovers	34	16	4	14	83	67	36
East Fife	34	15	4	15	85	71	34
King's Park	34	13	8	13	85	80	34
Dumbarton	34	14	6	14	69	67	34
Arbroath	34	14	5	15	65	62	33
Alloa Athletic	34	14	5	15	60	58	33
St Bernard's	34	13	6	15	67	64	32
Dundee Utd	34	14	4	16	65	67	32
Forfar Athletic	34	12	4	18	68	87	28
Brechin City	34	11	4	19	65	95	26
Leith Athletic	34	10	5	19	43	81	25
Montrose	34	8	5	21	63	89	21
Edinburgh City	34	4	4	26	39	133	12
*Armadale							
*Bo'ness							

*Armadale and Bo'ness expelled and their results expunged.

13 Aug	H	Dundee United	2–0 W
20 Aug	A	Albion Rovers	2–0 L
24 Aug	H	Montrose	4–1 W
27 Aug	H	East Fife	2–1 W
3 Sep	A	Dunfermline Athletic	2–2 D

10 Sep	H	Leith Athletic	3–0 W
15 Sep	A	Armadale	4–2* W
17 Sep	A	Brechin City	4–2 W
24 Sep	H	King's Park	1–0 L
1 Oct	A	Arbroath	3–0 W
8 Oct	H	Bo'ness	7–0* W
15 Oct	A	Edinburgh City	4–0 W
22 Oct	A	Alloa Athletic	3–0 W
29 Oct	H	Raith Rovers	2–1 W
5 Nov	A	Montrose	3–1 W
12 Nov	H	Armadale	8–2* W
19 Nov	A	St Bernard's	1–0 W
26 Nov	H	Stenhousemuir	4–1 W
3 Dec	A	Dumbarton	3–2 L
10 Dec	A	Queen of the South	0–0 D
17 Dec	H	Forfar Athletic	2–0 W
24 Dec	A	Dundee United	2–0 W
31 Dec	H	Albion Rovers	2–1 W
2 Jan	A	Leith Athletic	1–0 W
3 Jan	H	Brechin City	3–1 W
7 Jan	A	East Fife	5–0 W
14 Jan	H	Dunfermline Athletic	3–1 W
28 Jan	A	King's Park	0–0 D
11 Feb	H	Arbroath	2–0 W
18 Feb	H	Edinburgh City	7–1 W
11 Mar	H	Alloa Athletic	1–0 W
18 Mar	A	Raith Rovers	2–1 W
29 Mar	H	St Bernard's	4–1 W
8 Apr	A	Stenhousemuir	3–2 L
15 Apr	H	Dumbarton	1–0 W
22 Apr	H	Queen of the South	2–1 L
29 Apr	A	Forfar Athletic	3–3 D

Appearances

| George Blyth | 36 |
| Hugh McFarlane | 35 |

Hector Wilkinson	34
Robert Wallace	33
Willie Watson	32
Michael Langton	31
Duncan Urquhart	31
Johnny Halligan	30
Rab Walls	27
Peter Flucker	27
Peter McPherson	16
John Polland	15
James Hart	13
Willie Clark	11
Patrick Connolly	9
Robert Marshall	7
Hugh Sharkey	7
Peter Carruthers	5
Alex Hutchison	3
Trialists	2
John Hill	1
John Cowie	1
Tom Trotter	1

Goals

Robert Wallace	22
Peter Flucker	20
Rab Walls	16
James Hart	13
Patrick Connolly	8
Peter McPherson	5
John Polland	3
Alex Hutchison	3
Willie Watson	2
Michael Langton	2
Johnny Halligan	2
Hugh McFarlane	1
Hugh Sharkey	1
Peter Carruthers	1

CHAMPIONS OF THE WORLD

As Scottish Cup winners in 1887, Hibernian met crack English side Preston North End for a game grandly described as for the 'Association Football Championship of the World'. In front of a record crowd at Easter Road, Hibs emerged victorious 2–1.

THE BROONS

Jock Brown was a talented goalkeeper who had shared the number one jersey during Hibernian's successful league championship campaign in 1947/48. Like so many of his compatriots, his career was interrupted by the war – he had been well established at Clyde prior to it and indeed won a Scotland cap in 1938.

He was to have two sons who both became internationals for Scotland too – but at Rugby. Gordon and Peter Brown were brilliant forwards for Scotland in the 1970s and Gordon was a double lion.

They weren't the only internationals in the family: Jock's brother Jim was also an international footballer – but for the United States, making them a rare example of international brothers playing for different countries.

Curiously, Jock Brown played alongside Willie Ormond who also had a brother Bert who played football for another country, in this case, New Zealand. Willie's nephews Iain and Duncan were also New Zealand internationals.

THEY SAID IT

'I don't have any regrets about not moving during my playing career. I was born a Hibee, my dad was a Hibee, I will stay a Hibee and I'll die a Hibee.'

Lawrie Reilly

BOSMAN

One of the most famous players to play at Easter Road was Jean-Marc Bosman who played for Liège in a 0–0 draw at Easter Road in 1989. He didn't feature in the return game at Liège when a Jean-François De Sart wonder strike sealed the game in extra time.

It was barely a year later that Bosman wanted to move to Dunkirk in the French leagues, but Dunkirk refused to pay Liège the transfer fee they were looking for. Liège then cut his wages, and Bosman took his case for restraint of trade to the European Court of Justice in Luxembourg. In December 1995, the court ruled in Bosman's favour meaning that players would be entitled to a free transfer at the end of their contracts.

This was to be a very significant move in football as prior to this clubs could withhold the registrations of players to prevent them moving on at the end of their contract.

THE FRENCH MANAGERS

Bosman isn't the first famous person to grace the Easter Road turf for opposition teams – two former France managers came up against Hibs in European compeitition.

Michel Hidalgo was a member of the Reims side that beat Hibs in the semi-finals of the inaugural European Cup. He masterminded France's 1984 European Championship victory before standing down.

Raymond Domenech was a member of the Strasbourg side that defeated Hibs in the UEFA Cup in 1978. After a successful spell at Lyon, he went on to become France manager from 2004 until 2010, leading them to the 2006 World Cup final and then leaving after a disastrous 2010 World Cup campaign where they finished bottom of their group.

BARCELONA, REAL MADRID

The Spanish giants are two of the most star-studded sides in the world, but both have been humbled on the Easter Road pitch, although these games didn't happen yesterday.

Firstly Barcelona pitched up at Easter Road for a UEFA Cup tie in February 1961. Hugh Shaw's team had managed to draw at the Nou Camp with goals from Tommy Preston, Johnny MacLeod and a Joe Baker double, so the return in Edinburgh was eagerly awaited.

The match was evenly poised at 2–2 heading into the final minutes after goals by Joe Baker and Tommy Preston. The referee awarded Hibs a penalty and it sparked a riot among the Barcelona players, the game being delayed for 13 minutes as the police had to move in for the referee's safety and to restore order. When calm prevailed, everyone expected the Hibs regular penalty taker Sammy Baird to step up to take the spot lick, but instead he gave the ball to Bobby Kinloch. It transpired that nerves had got the better of him and during the 13-minute delay he had an accident in his shorts.

In front of 45,000 Kinloch stroked the ball home to ensure victory for the home side and a bonus of £90 which was a lot of money in those days.

The Hibs team for this game was Simpson, Fraser, McClelland, Baxter, Easton, Baird, MacLeod, Preston, Baker, Kinloch and Ormond.

Lately, Hibs met Barcelona in a friendly at Murrayfield in 2008. Hibs fared slightly worse this time being beaten 6–0. That, however, turned out to be the Barcelona side that lifted every trophy available to them and rounded it all off by becoming World Club champions.

Real Madrid arrived in October 1964 to play a friendly. Real had dominated the early years of the European Cup and many of the team that faced Hibs would go on to lift the European Cup again in 1966. The Hibernian manager for this game was Jock Stein and the players in action were:

Wilson, Fraser, Parke, Stanton, McNamee, Baxter, Cormack, Hamilton, Scott, Quinn and Martin. The unused substitutes were Eric Stevenson and Jimmy O'Rourke.

In front of a crowd of 30,000 Hibs were superb, and Willie Hamilton was at his untouchable best. They scored through the teenage Peter Cormack and Zoco scored an own goal to give Hibernian a 2–0 victory. They wore green shorts on this occasion as a contrast to the all-white Real Madrid strip and were to reprise this kit in several seasons from 2004 onwards.

CONSECUTIVE GAMES

Joe Davis played 273 consecutive games for Hibernian after joining from Third Lanark in 1964. Of these games 243 were competitive. His run started in December 1964 in a 2–1 victory at Partick Thistle when he replaced Tommy Leishman and only ended in September 1969 when he lost his place to Mervyn Jones for a league game against St Mirren.

LEGENDS – PAT STANTON

Stanton is regarded by many Hibs fans as the greatest player they ever saw. He was born in Edinburgh in 1944, and started his career at Bonnyrigg Rose where he shone in the Scottish Junior Cup before making his Hibernian debut in a 4–3 defeat at Motherwell in 1963 as a 19-year-old, netting in that game. He established himself in the team straight away and was to remain a fixture for the following 13 years. It's no surprise as Pat actually had impeccable Hibee credentials as Michael Whelahan and Jimmy Hendren were ancestors.

Pat was to enjoy many highs at Hibernian including some great European results as well as scoring against Celtic in the League Cup final win of 1972. His lowest point was possibly when he missed the penalty in the shoot-out against Leeds that allowed the Yorkshiremen to steal victory.

Pat was a regular Scotland international too, winning 16 caps over an 8-year period, and captaining the side on 3 occasions. He made his final Hibs appearance as a substitute against St Johnstone in a sectional League Cup tie in August 1976. He moved on to Celtic, where he won the league and the Scottish Cup under Jock Stein. Hibs' average league attendance dropped 3,000 in the season after he left – a reduction of 25 per cent.

He moved on to Aberdeen as Sir Alex Ferguson's assistant before he moved on to Cowdenbeath and Dunfermline. He returned to Easter Road in 1982 to assume the manager's role after Bertie Auld have been relieved of his duties following a period of putrid football. Sadly, it didn't work out and Pat resigned two years later after a home defeat to Dumbarton left Hibs stranded at the bottom of the league table. He presided over some dreadful cup defeats as well, although his time did lay the foundations for better days as Gordon Hunter, Mickey Weir and Paul Kane were all to make their breakthroughs under his charge.

After leaving Hibernian Pat didn't work in football again, but has latterly returned to Easter Road as a matchday host along with Lawrie Reilly. Pat made 617 appearances for Hibs scoring 78 goals. He won the League Cup in 1972 and the Drybrough Cup in 1972 and 1973. He played in the sides which finished runners-up in the Scottish Cup in 1972 and the League Cup in 1968 and 1974.

Pat managed Hibs for 91 games, winning 25, drawing 26 and losing 40. His first game in charge was on 4 September 1982 in a game that finished 0–0 at Easter Road at home to St Mirren. Only Jim McArthur, Erich Schaedler and Arthur Duncan remained from the team he left just six years earlier along with his replacement Jackie McNamara. Pat was an inaugural inductee to the Hibs Hall of Fame.

FAMOUS FANS

Hibs have more than their fair share of celebrity fans, among them actor Dougray Scott who starred in *Mission Impossible II* and *Enigma*. Also in the entertainment field are the Proclaimers; twins Craig and Charlie Reid who once performed before a Champions League final when it was contested at Hampden in 2002. Singer Fish is another who has followed Hibs for a number of years.

In the world of politics current MSP Margo MacDonald is a fan as well as past MSPs Brian Monteith and Lloyd Quinan. Scott Hastings, who was once the most capped Scotsman at the other football code, rugby is another Hibee.

Media brothers Grant Stott and John Leslie, as well as *Trainspotting* writer Irvine Welsh have also been regular attendees at Easter Road.

CHAMPIONS V – 1947/48

When Willie McCartney had taken over at Hibs, after a near miss with relegation in 1936, he set about a clear plan to make the club great again. Ultimately, by a cruel twist of fate he was not to see the glory of work.

McCartney had an eye for a player, and he set about overhauling the Easter Road squad and replacing them with younger, promising players who would ultimately gel into a team who would win three league championships. The nucleus of the 'Famous Five' had come into place, along with Bobby Combe who covered all the forward positions as well as a few behind them as well. Lawrie Reilly was yet to reach his promise and played just six games in the championship season.

Hibs won the title on 3 May 1948, after completing their programme when Hearts beat Rangers in the final game, not that there was much chance of Rangers overhauling them due to Hibernian's superior goal average. McCartney was not to live long enough to witness the triumph as he died after a Scottish Cup tie at Coatbridge in January. Hugh Shaw took over to guide the club safely to the title.

	P	W	D	L	F	A	Pts
Hibernian	30	22	4	4	86	27	48
Rangers	30	21	4	5	64	28	46
Partick Thistle	30	16	4	10	61	42	36
Dundee	30	15	3	12	67	51	33
St Mirren	30	13	5	12	54	58	31
Clyde	30	12	7	11	52	57	31
Falkirk	30	10	10	10	55	48	30
Motherwell	30	13	3	14	45	47	29
Hearts	30	10	8	12	37	42	28
Aberdeen	30	10	7	13	45	45	27
Third Lanark	30	10	6	14	56	73	26
Celtic	30	10	5	15	41	56	25
Queen of the South	30	10	5	15	49	74	25
Morton	30	9	6	15	47	43	24
Airdrie	30	7	7	16	40	78	21
Queen's Park	30	9	2	19	45	75	20

13 Aug	A	Aberdeen	2–0 W
27 Aug	H	Airdrieonians	7–1 W
20 Sep	A	Hearts	2–1 L
27 Sep	H	Clyde	2–1 W
4 Oct	A	Queen's Park	3–2 W
11 Oct	H	Queen of the South	6–0 W
18 Oct	A	Rangers	2–1 L
25 Oct	H	Morton	1–1 D
1 Nov	A	Motherwell	2–0 W
8 Nov	H	Third Lanark	8–0 W
15 Nov	H	Dundee	2–1 W
22 Nov	A	Falkirk	3–1 L
29 Nov	H	St Mirren	5–0 W

6 Dec	A	Partick Thistle	1–1 D
13 Dec	H	Celtic	1–1 D
20 Dec	H	Aberdeen	4–0 W
27 Dec	A	Airdrieonians	3–0 W
1 Jan	H	Hearts	3–1 W
3 Jan	A	Clyde	2–2 D
10 Jan	H	Queen's Park	4–0 W
17 Jan	A	Queen of the South	3–0 W
31 Jan	H	Rangers	1–0 W
14 Feb	A	Morton	2–1 W
28 Feb	A	Third Lanark	4–1 W
13 Mar	H	Falkirk	2–0 W
20 Mar	A	St Mirren	4–2 W
3 Apr	A	Celtic	4–2 W
17 Apr	H	Partick Thistle	1–0 W
19 Apr	H	Motherwell	5–0 W
1 May	A	Dundee	3–1 L

Appearances

Jock Govan	29
Archie Buchanan	29
Gordon Smith	29
Bobby Combe	29
Davie Shaw	28
Alex Linwood	24
Eddie Turnbull	23
Willie Ormond	23
Hugh Howie	17
Willie Finnegan	15
Sammy Kean	13
Jimmy Kerr	12
Jock Brown	11
Peter Aird	9
Jock Cuthbertson	9
Simon Waldie	8
George Farm	7

Lawrie Reilly	6
Leslie Johnstone	4
Johnny Aitkenhead	4
Jimmy Cairns	1

Goals

Gordon Smith	19
Alex Linwood	14
Willie Ormond	12
Eddie Turnbull	11
Jock Cuthbertson	10
Bobby Combe	8
Leslie Johnstone	5
Lawrie Reilly	4
Archie Buchanan	1
Johnny Aitkenhead	1

YOUNG GUNS

The youngest player to represent Hibs in a first-team game was Jamie McCluskey who was 16 years and 79 days old when he made his debut as a substitute against Kilmarnock in the SPL on 24 January 2004. Hibs won 2–0 through goals from Scott Brown and Garry O'Connor. McCluskey made 28 appearances, scoring a single penalty goal before being released in 2007. The top ten youngest players to have made their Hibernian debuts are as follows:

Jamie McCluskey	16y 79d	v Kilmarnock	Jan 2004
Jimmy O'Rourke	16y 85d	v DOS Utrecht	Dec 1962
Peter Cormack	16y 130d	v Airdrieonians	Nov 1962
Gordon Hunter	16y 190d	v Kilmarnock	Nov 1983
Derek McWilliams	16y 214d	v Clydebank	Aug 1982
Kevin McKee	16y 268d	v Rangers	Mar 1983
James Kane	16y 300d	v Livingston	Apr 2004

Brian Rice	16y 331d	v Motherwell	Sep 1980
Alex McGhee	16y 332d	v Rangers	Apr 1972
Gordon Smith	16y 338d	v Hearts	Apr 1941

The youngest Scottish Cup debutant is Jimmy O'Rourke who was 16 years and 130 days old when he played against Brechin City in January 1963.

The youngest first-team goalscorer was also Jimmy O'Rourke when he scored against Dunfermline Athletic in a Scottish League game in December 1962 aged just 16 years and 88 days. Hibs lost the game 3–2.

THE OLD GUARD

The oldest player to represent Hibs in a first-team game was John Burridge when he played his final game for Hibs aged 41 years and 163 days old against Partick Thistle on 15 May 1993. Hibs lost 1–0 and this game brought the curtain down on his Hibs career, after 77 games, which included the Skol Cup final in 1991. He had signed from Newcastle United and left for Scarborough and his career continued for a while after leaving Hibs. The ten oldest players to have played for Hibs are as follows:

John Burridge	41y 163d	v Partick Thistle	May 1993
Ray Wilkins	40y 112d	v Rangers	Jan 1997
Jim Leighton	38y 302d	v Airdrieonians	May 1997
Alex Hall	38y 207d	v Morton	Jan 1947
Jimmy McColl	38y 132d	v Falkirk	Apr 1931
Ally Donaldson	37y 272d	v Celtic	Aug 1981
Mark Venus	37y 169d	v Albion Rovers	Sep 2004
Joe McLaughlin	36y 342d	v Raith Rovers	May 1997
Arthur Duncan	36y 124d	v Dundee United	Apr 1984
Willie Finnegan	36y 87d	v Rangers	Feb 1949

The oldest first-team goalscorer was Jimmy McColl when he scored against Cowdenbeath in a Scottish League game in February 1931 aged 38 years and 55 days old.

FLOODLIGHT PIONEERS

On 7 November 1951, Hibs played in the first game in Scotland to be staged under floodlights, a friendly against Stenhousemuir. The game finished 5–3 to Hibs.

Hibs were also in action in the first floodlit competitive match when they entertained Raith Rovers in a Scottish Cup tie on 8 February 1956. The sides drew 1–1 with Eddie Turnbull scoring the Hibs goal in front of a healthy midweek crowd of 26,024.

SCORING GOALKEEPER

The only goalkeeper to have ever scored for Hibs in a bona fide first-team game is Andy Goram. He made 163 appearances in goal for Hibs between 1987 and 1991. In a game against Morton in May 1988, he opened the scoring with a kick out which sailed past the unfortunate David Wylie in goal for the already relegated visitors. Hibs went on to win 3–1.

Goram also scored in a penalty shoot-out – in the third round of the League Cup in August 1989. Clydebank had held Hibs to a 0–0 draw after extra time, but went on to lose 5–3 on penalties to the Edinburgh side.

RELEGATION

Hibs have been relegated three times in their history, and this has resulted in playing in Scotland's second tier for four seasons. They were relegated in 1930/31, 1979/80 and most recently in 1997/98. They bounced back to the top division at the first time of asking in both 1980 and 1998, but they required two bites at the cherry to achieve promotion in the 1930s, winning the Second Division in 1932/33.

FAMOUS FIVE

Hibernian's most celebrated forward line was the post-war line-up of Gordon Smith, Bobby Johnstone, Lawrie Reilly, Eddie Turnbull and Willie Ormond. All were internationals, and all scored 100 league goals for Hibs – only two other players have managed this in Hibs history.

The quintet made their collective debut in a friendly game at Nithsdale Wanderers on 21 April 1949, a match that Hibs won 8–1. It was to be some months before they played together competitively, when Hibs beat Queen of the South 2–0 in October.

In total, they scored an eye-watering 1,074 goals in their Hibernian careers between them. The last time they were to play together was at home to Clyde on 29 January 1955, a match which they surprisingly lost 3–2 although Ormond and Reilly scored.

On one single occasion all played and scored in a competitive game – v Clyde in the Scottish Cup in February 1954. Hibs won 7–0 in front of just under 20,000 spectators.

The North Stand was renamed the Famous Five Stand in 1998 in their honour.

HAT-TRICKS

Since 1900, no fewer than 217 hat-tricks have been scored in Hibernian colours – one 9-goal haul, three 5s, thirty 4s and 183 trebles. Joe Baker was the man who notched the 9 against Peebles Rovers in a Scottish Cup game in February 1961.

The fives were scored by Peter Flucker against Vale of Atholl in the Scottish Cup in January 1935, Gordon Smith against Third Lanark in November 1947, and Joe Baker also against Third Lanark in December 1960.

The men who notched the most hat-tricks are unsurprisingly the club record scorers; Gordon Smith and Lawrie Reilly both managed 18 each, just ahead of Joe Baker who managed 16 in his four years at the club before he moved on to Italian side Torino.

The youngest hat-trick scorer is Gordon Smith who scored a treble on debut in a wartime Southern Leauge game against Hearts in April 1941, aged just 16 years and 338 days. Hibs won 5–3, and Tommy Walker on the losing side also scored a hat-trick.

Joe Harper managed to score a hat-trick in a Hibs side that was still beaten by three clear goals. His trio came at Hampden in the League Cup final of 1974 against Celtic but Hibs still lost 6–3. Dixie Deans scored a hat-trick for Celtic that day.

LOWEST CROWD

Hibs drew their lowest crowd of modern times against Stirling Albion on 23 March 1955, when just 875 people turned up to watch a league game. Just two days earlier, 24,000 had turned up for a floodlit fixture against Arsenal, but against Stirling the floodlights stayed off and the match kicked off at 5 p.m. on a Wednesday evening.

HALFWAY-LINE GOAL

Hibernian fans had learned to expect the unexpected when Chic Charnley joined the club, and while they weren't treated to his legendary indiscipline, they did get to see him in a purple patch in the summer of 1997. He demonstrated this admirably by scoring from inside his own half in a League Cup tie against Alloa Athletic, a game in which Hibs won 3–1. Chico being Chico, he didn't take the easy way of scoring down the slope – oh no, he scored up it. Sadly there were no television cameras to capture the event. Barry Lavety, and Pat McGinlay were the other Hibernian scorers that day.

TESTIMONIALS

Since the Second World War the following players have received testimonials for their long service:

15 Sep 1952	Gordon Smith	Hibs 7–3 Man Utd
15 Dec 1958	Lawrie Reilly	Hibs 9–3 International Select
30 Apr 1978	Pat Stanton	Hibs 2–1 Celtic
3 May 1981	Arthur Duncan	Hibs 3–4 International Select
5 Aug 1984	Jackie McNamara	Hibs 0–3 Newcastle
3 Oct 1988	Gordon Rae	Hibs 0–3 Man Utd
14 Oct 1991	Alan Sneddon	Hibs 4–2 Aston Villa
9 Sep 1996	Gordon Hunter	Hibs 3–2 Coventry
3 Sep 2011	Ian Murray	Hibs 5–5 Hibs Legends

Kenny Dalglish played for Hibs in the Alan Sneddon testimonial, while World Cup winners Robert Pires and Patrick Vieira played for Hibs in the Ian Murray match.

Gordon Strachan played for Hibernian in October 2002, when they took on Falkirk in a testimonial for winger Kevin McAllister who had graced both clubs.

LEGENDS – BOBBY JOHNSTONE

Bobby Johnstone was the inside-right of the Famous Five forward line. The youngest, he was the final piece of the jigsaw, but also the first to leave when he departed for Manchester City.

Born in Selkirk in 1929, Bobby made his debut at St Mirren in a 2–0 defeat in 1949. It was September that year that he scored his first goal, against Partick Thistle, before going on to establish himself as part of the Five. He was a key member of the group, and enjoyed his best season in 1951/52 when he scored 29 goals in 40 games. He made his debut for Scotland against England at Wembley in 1951 scoring in a 3–2 win.

Johnstone moved on to Manchester City in 1955, where he was to play alongside future Hibs manager Dave Ewing. He scored in consecutive FA Cup finals, winning the trophy in 1956. He later returned to Hibs in 1959, scoring in his penultimate game against Airdrie in a 6–1 win. He made his final appearance for Hibs the following week in a 3–1 defeat at Tannadice after which he moved on to Oldham Athletic.

Bobby played 263 games for Hibs scoring 142 goals. For Scotland he scored 10 goals in 17 games. He won two league championships at Hibs, and an FA Cup winner's medal with Manchester City. He was an original inductee to the Hibs Hall of Fame and was inducted into the Scottish Football Hall of Fame in 2010.

CHAMPIONS VI – 1950/51

Hibs regained the league title in 1951, as they dominated the competition, winning by 10 clear points over Rangers. However, after three games they had just two points and it took an excellent run of eight wins in a row to provide the platform for the victory.

By 1950, the Famous Five were well established and between them they contributed 67 of Hibs' 78 goals. It wasn't just the strikers who earned the plaudits either – Tommy Younger was an excellent goalkeeper and Jock Paterson was a talented half-back who would surely have won international honours if he hadn't been born on the wrong side of Hadrian's Wall. As part of a solid defensive unit they conceded just 26 goals in 30 games.

Hibernian won the title emphatically with a 4–0 win at Clyde on 11 April with four games still to play.

	P	W	D	L	F	A	Pts
Hibernian	30	22	4	4	78	26	48
Rangers	30	17	4	9	64	37	38
Dundee	30	15	8	7	47	30	38
Hearts	30	16	5	9	72	45	37
Aberdeen	30	15	5	10	61	50	35
Partick Thistle	30	13	7	10	57	48	33
Celtic	30	12	5	13	48	46	29
Raith Rovers	30	13	2	15	52	52	28
Motherwell	30	11	6	13	58	65	28
East Fife	30	10	8	12	48	66	28
St Mirren	30	9	7	14	35	51	25
Morton	30	10	4	16	47	59	24
Third Lanark	30	11	2	17	40	51	24
Airdrie	30	10	4	16	52	67	24
Clyde	30	8	7	15	37	57	23
Falkirk	30	7	4	19	35	81	18

9 Sep	H	Falkirk	6–0 W
23 Sep	H	Hearts	1–0 L
30 Sep	A	Aberdeen	2–1 L
14 Oct	A	Motherwell	6–2 W
4 Nov	A	Rangers	1–1 D
11 Nov	H	Morton	2–0 W
18 Nov	A	East Fife	2–1 W

25 Nov	H	Airdrieonians	5–0 W
2 Dec	H	Dundee	2–0 W
9 Dec	A	Third Lanark	2–1 W
16 Dec	H	St Mirren	3–1 W
23 Dec	A	Falkirk	5–1 W
30 Dec	H	Clyde	1–0 W
1 Jan	A	Hearts	2–1 L
2 Jan	H	Aberdeen	6–2 W
6 Jan	A	Raith Rovers	3–1 W
13 Jan	H	Motherwell	3–1 W
20 Jan	H	Partick Thistle	1–1 D
3 Feb	A	Celtic	1–0 W
17 Feb	A	Morton	4–2 W
24 Feb	H	East Fife	2–0 W
3 Mar	A	Airdrieonians	2–1 L
17 Mar	H	Third Lanark	3–1 W
24 Mar	A	St Mirren	1–0 W
7 Apr	A	Dundee	2–2 D
11 Apr	A	Clyde	4–0 W
21 Apr	A	Partick Thistle	0–0 D
25 Apr	H	Raith Rovers	3–0 W
28 Apr	H	Rangers	4–1 W
30 Apr	H	Celtic	3–1 W

Appearances

Jock Paterson	30
Tommy Younger	29
Bobby Johnstone	29
Lawrie Reilly	29
Bobby Combe	27
Archie Buchanan	27
Eddie Turnbull	25
Gordon Smith	25
Jock Govan	24
Willie Ormond	23
John Ogilvie	23
Hugh Howie	13

Jimmy Cairns	7
Robert Wood	5
Michael Gallacher	4
Jimmy Mulkerrin	2
Jimmy Souness	2
Jimmy Gunning	1
Willie Allan	1
Pat Ward	1
Lawrie Higgins	1
Willie Bruce	1
John Munro	1

Goals

Lawrie Reilly	23
Eddie Turnbull	15
Bobby Johnstone	12
Gordon Smith	10
Willie Ormond	7
Archie Buchanan	4
Bobby Combe	3
Robert Wood	2
Jimmy Souness	2

JUST ONE GAME

The story of Willie Adam is scarcely believable, but he only played a single game in his senior football career and that was in the European Cup.

In 1955 Hibernian were Scotland's first entrants into Europe, and drawn against the West German champions Rot-Weiss Essen. Hibs had comfortably seen off their hosts in the first leg 4–0, but for the return leg travel issues meant that first choice goalkeeper Tommy Younger was missing. Instead, Hibs called in teenage understudy Willie Adam who had signed from Ormiston Primrose. The replacement performed admirably as Hibs saw out a 1–1 draw to qualify for the next round. However, that was to be his only senior appearance and he was released shortly afterwards.

PENALTY SHOOT-OUTS

Hibs have an enviable record in penalty shoot-outs having never lost to a Scottish side. There is one blot on their copybook, however, a loss to Leeds United in their very first competitive shoot-out in 1973, Pat Stanton missing the decisive spot kick. Their complete record is as follows:

November 1973, v Leeds United, lost 5–4
Alex Cropley, John Blackley, Des Bremner and John Hazel scored, but Pat Stanton missed.

September 1985, v Celtic, won 4–3
Iain Munro, Gordon Durie, Mark Fulton and Stevie Cowan scored while Gordon Rae and Ally Brazil missed.

August 1989, v Clydebank, won 5–3
Paul Kane, John Collins, Keith Houchen, Neil Orr and Andy Goram scored.

August 1993, v Partick Thistle, won 3–2
Michael O'Neill, Keith Wright and Darren Jackson scored, while Tom McIntyre and Billy Findlay missed.

January 1997, v Aberdeen, won 5–4
Pat McGinlay, Shaun Dennis, Ian Cameron, Brian Grant and Kevin Harper scored.

August 1999, v Clyde, won 5–4
Stuart Lovell, Kenny Miller, Pat McGinlay, Stevie Crawford and Russell Latapy scored.

February 2004, v Rangers, won 4–3
Gary Caldwell, Scott Brown, Tam McManus and Colin Murdock scored, while Stephen Dobbie, Garry O'Connor and Mathias Doumbé missed.

September 2011, v Motherwell, Hibs won 7–6
Garry O'Connor, Victor Palsson, Junior Agogo, Leigh Griffiths, Sean O'Hanlon, David Wotherspoon and Richie Towell scored, while Callum Booth missed.

Ian Cameron missed a penalty for Partick Thistle in the 1993 shoot-out, but scored in the 1997 meeting.

LEGENDS – LAWRIE REILLY

Lawrie Reilly was the heavy scoring centre forward at the hub of the Famous Five forward line. Born in Edinburgh in 1928, he made his debut for Hibs against Kilmarnock in October 1945 and scored his first goal for the side the following month. He was the only one of the Five to brought up as a Hibs fan.

A prolific centre forward, he quickly established himself in the Scotland team of the era, and to this day no Hibee has played for their country more often while with the club. He played in three league championship winning sides, and scored 22 goals in 38 Scotland appearances. He didn't have much luck with injuries, however, and retired from playing before his 30th birthday. He also missed out on playing in a World Cup.

Reilly made his final appearance for Hibs in a 3–1 victory over Rangers in which, naturally, he scored.

Lawrie scored 6 goals for Scotland in 7 appearances against England, and his timing earned him the nickname 'Last minute Lawrie' due to the lateness with which he often struck.

He made 355 appearances for Hibs, scoring 238 goals – only Gordon Smith scored more. His best season for Hibs was in 1952/53 when he scored 46 goals in 46 games.

He is a member of the Hibs Hall of Fame, and the Scottish Football Hall of Fame.

GROUNDS

Hibernian have played home games on five different grounds. When first formed, in common with a lot of other Edinburgh clubs, they played at the Meadows. They then moved on to Powderhall in 1878, before relocating to Mayfield a year later. They then moved on to Easter Road, but not the current ground – it was 1893 before they moved into their current location, and despite the subsequent threat of moves to Straiton since, they have remained there ever since.

THE INTERNATIONAL SET

The players who have won international caps while playing for Hibs are as follows:

Algeria	Abderraouf Zarabi	1 caps 0 goals
Australia	Stuart Lovell	2 caps 0 goals
Austria	Alen Orman	1 caps 0 goals
Canada	Paul Fenwick	18 caps 0 goals
DR Congo	Yves Ma-Kalambay	1 caps 0 goals
Ecuador	Ulises De La Cruz	16 caps 1 goal
England	Joe Baker	5 caps 1 goal
Finland	Jonatan Johansson	5 caps 3 goals
	Mixu Paatelainen	11 caps 3 goals
	Jarkko Wiss	2 caps 0 goals
Gambia	Pa Saikou Kujabi	3 caps 0 goals
Iceland	Ólafur Gottskálksson	2 caps 0 goals

Ireland FAI	Paddy Farrell	2 caps 0 goals
Ireland IFA	Paddy Farrell	1 caps 0 goals
	Bill Gowdy	1 caps 0 goals
	Jack Jones	4 caps 0 goals
Ivory Coast	Souleymane Bamba	17 caps 2 goals
Morocco	Abdessalam Benjelloun	9 caps 3 goals
	Merouane Zemmama	7 caps 1 goal
New Zealand	Chris Killen	4 caps 1 goal
Northern Ireland	Colin Murdock	7 caps 1 goal
	Michael O'Neill	7 caps 3 goals
	John Parke	2 caps 0 goals
	Dean Shiels	8 caps 0 goals
	Ivan Sproule	8 caps 1 goal
Republic of Ireland	Nick Colgan	8 caps 0 goals
	Mike Gallagher	1 caps 0 goals
	Liam Miller	1 caps 0 goals
Scotland	John Blackley	7 caps 0 goals
	Des Bremner	1 caps 0 goals
	Barney Breslin	1 caps 0 goals
	Scott Brown	3 caps 0 goals
	John Brownlie	7 caps 0 goals
	Gary Caldwell	16 caps 1 goal
	Paddy Callaghan	1 caps 0 goals
	John Collins	4 caps 1 goal
	Bobby Combe	3 caps 1 goal
	Peter Cormack	4 caps 0 goals
	Alec Cropley	2 caps 0 goals
	Arthur Duncan	6 caps 0 goals
	Jimmy Dunn	5 caps 1 goal
	Stephen Fletcher	4 caps 1 goal
	Bobby Glen	1 caps 0 goals
	Andy Goram	11 caps 0 goals
	Jock Govan	6 caps 0 goals
	John Grant	2 caps 0 goals
	Archie Gray	1 caps 0 goals
	Willie Groves	1 caps 1 goal

Scotland	Willie Hamilton	1 caps 0 goals
	Joe Harper	1 caps 1 goal
	Willie Harper	9 caps 0 goals
	Hugh Howie	1 caps 1 goal
	Darren Jackson	20 caps 3 goals
	Bobby Johnstone	13 caps 8 goals
	John Kennedy	1 caps 0 goals
	Peter Kerr	1 caps 0 goals
	Jim Leighton	23 caps 0 goals
	Jimmy Lundie	1 caps 0 goals
	Jimmy Main	1 caps 0 goals
	Neil Martin	2 caps 0 goals
	Billy McCartney	1 caps 0 goals
	Jimmy McGhee	1 caps 0 goals
	J. McLaren	1 caps 0 goals
	Johnny McLeod	4 caps 0 goals
	Murdo McLeod	3 caps 0 goals
	Ian Murray	3 caps 0 goals
	Paddy Murray	2 caps 1 goal
	Bobby Neil	1 caps 2 goals
	Willie Ormond	6 caps 2 goals
	Garry O'Connor	7 caps 1 goal
	John O'Neil	1 caps 0 goals
	Lawrie Reilly	38 caps 22 goals
	Harry Rennie	11 caps 0 goals
	Derek Riordan	3 caps 0 goals
	Harry Ritchie	2 caps 0 goals
	William Robb	1 caps 0 goals
	Alan Rough	2 caps 0 goals
	Erich Schaedler	1 caps 0 goals
	Jim Scott	1 caps 0 goals
	Davie Shaw	9 caps 0 goals
	Gordon Smith	19 caps 4 goals
	Pat Stanton	16 caps 0 goals
	George Stewart	2 caps 0 goals
	Eddie Turnbull	9 caps 0 goals

Scotland	Duncan Urquhart	1 caps 0 goals
	Keith Wright	1 caps 0 goals
	Tommy Younger	8 caps 0 goals
St Lucia	Earl Jean	1 caps 0 goals
Trinidad & Tobago	Lyndon Andrews	13 caps 0 goals
	Russell Latapy	23 caps 4 goals
	Tony Rougier	8 caps 0 goals
Wales	Bobby Atherton	5 caps 0 goals

EUROPEAN CUP RUN

Hibs were Scotland's, and Britain's, first representatives in Europe when they competed in the inaugural European Cup in 1955. The competition was intended for league champions and it is a matter of some conjecture as to why Hibs were invited ahead of Aberdeen who were the Scottish champions at the time; some reports suggest a lack of interest from Aberdeen while others say it was Hibs' floodlights which were necessary for the midweek games that it would entail.

Hibs started their campaign in Germany against West German champions Rot-Weiss Essen and recorded a superb 4–0 victory before a 1–1 draw at Easter Road saw them safely through.

In the next round, the quarter-final, they were drawn against Swedish representatives Djurgårdens who had seen off Gardia Warsaw in the first round. Hibs had a bit of luck; the away leg was rescheduled for Firhill due to the severity of the Swedish winter and Hibs responded by emerging victorious 3–1. The home leg was safely negotiated to set up a semi-final with French side Reims with the victors progressing to the very first European Cup final where they would meet Real Madrid.

Unfortunately a very good French side – with several players who would perform with distinction in the 1958 World Cup – managed to beat Hibs 2–0 in their home leg. Hibernian were unable to overturn the advantage down the slope in the second, as they slipped to a 1–0 defeat on the night and a 3–0 aggregate victory.

Hibs also made the semi-finals of the old Fairs Cup, where they would play a third match before losing to Roma. If current rules on away goals had applied then, they would have made the final.

MOST APPEARANCES

In all competitions these are the top ten Hibs players in the list:

Gordon Smith	636
Arthur Duncan	626
Pat Stanton	617
Willie Ormond	506
Eddie Turnbull	487
Peter Kerr	484
Bobby Combe	467
Johnny Halligan	457
Matt Paterson	445
Erich Schaedler	434

DIRECT FROM A CORNER

Paul Kane scored direct from a corner when Hibernian met Dundee at Easter Road in November 1985. Hibs won 2–1 in front of 6,474 fans, with Gordon Durie scoring the other goal that day.

HAT-TRICK OF PENALTIES

Eddie Turnbull scored a hat-trick of penalties in a game against Celtic in February 1950 as Hibs won 4–1, with Turnbull netting their other goal that day too. Bobby Collins scored for Celtic, with a penalty.

MOST GOALS

The all-important top ten in the list of leading goalscorers for Hibs in all competitions is as follows:

Gordon Smith	303
Lawrie Reilly	238
Eddie Turnbull	202
Willie Ormond	189
Joe Baker	158
Jimmy McColl	143
Bobby Johnstone	142
Jock Cuthbertson	124
Jimmy O'Rourke	122
Arthur Duncan	114

CHAMPIONS VII – 1951/52

Hibs retained the league title, for the only time in their history with essentially the same squad as the previous season. While the team wasn't as miserly as the season before, they did rack up 92 goals this time around with the Famous Five contributing 78 of them.

Hibs clinched the title without kicking a ball on this occasion, as Rangers' draw with Third Lanark on 16 April meant that the Ibrox side couldn't catch them.

	P	W	D	L	F	A	Pts
Hibernian	30	20	5	5	92	36	45
Rangers	30	16	9	5	61	31	41
East Fife	30	17	3	10	71	49	37
Hearts	30	14	7	9	69	53	35
Raith Rovers	30	14	5	11	43	42	33
Partick Thistle	30	12	7	11	48	51	31
Motherwell	30	12	7	11	51	57	31
Dundee	30	11	6	13	53	52	28
Celtic	30	10	8	12	52	55	28
Queen of South	30	10	8	12	50	60	28
Aberdeen	30	10	7	13	65	58	27
Third Lanark	30	9	8	13	51	62	26
Airdrie	30	11	4	15	54	69	26
St Mirren	30	10	5	15	43	58	25
Morton	30	9	6	15	49	56	24
Stirling Albion	30	5	5	20	36	99	15

8 Sep	A	Raith Rovers	2–0 W
15 Sep	H	Aberdeen	4–4 D
22 Sep	A	Hearts	1–1 D
29 Sep	H	Third Lanark	5–2 W
6 Oct	A	Stirling Albion	4–1 W
13 Oct	H	Morton	1–0 W
20 Oct	H	Partick Thistle	5–0 W
27 Oct	A	Celtic	1–1 D
3 Nov	H	Rangers	1–1 D
10 Nov	A	Morton	2–1 L
17 Nov	H	East Fife	4–2 W
24 Nov	A	Airdrieonians	2–0 W
1 Dec	A	Dundee	4–1 W
8 Dec	H	Queen of the South	5–0 W
15 Dec	A	St Mirren	4–0 W
22 Dec	H	Raith Rovers	5–0 W
29 Dec	A	Motherwell	3–1 L
1 Jan	H	Hearts	3–2 L

2 Jan	A	Third Lanark	5–0 W
5 Jan	H	Stirling Albion	8–0 W
12 Jan	A	Aberdeen	2–1 W
19 Jan	A	Partick Thistle	2–1 W
2 Feb	H	Celtic	3–1 W
13 Feb	A	Rangers	2–2 D
16 Feb	H	St Mirren	5–0 W
23 Feb	A	East Fife	3–1 L
1 Mar	H	Airdrieonians	4–0 W
15 Mar	A	Queen of the South	5–2 L
9 Apr	H	Dundee	3–1 W
21 Apr	H	Motherwell	3–1 W

Appearances

Jock Govan	30
Hugh Howie	30
Jock Paterson	30
Gordon Smith	29
Lawrie Reilly	29
Eddie Turnbull	29
Bobby Combe	27
Bobby Johnstone	27
Archie Buchanan	25
Tommy Younger	24
Willie Ormond	20
Michael Gallacher	19
Jimmy Kerr	4
Pat Ward	3
Willie Bruce	2
Jimmy Mulkerrin	1
Jimmy Souness	1

Goals

Lawrie Reilly	27
Bobby Johnstone	23
Willie Ormond	13

Bobby Combe	12
Gordon Smith	9
Eddie Turnbull	6
Archie Buchanan	2

LEGENDS – WILLIE ORMOND

Willie Ormond was a fast and skilful winger and a member of the Famous Five who joined Hibs from Stenhousemuir in 1946. He made his debut against Queen of the South in the following December, marking his first game with a goal in a 3–1 victory at Palmerston. He was to play for Hibs for the next 15 years.

Like Joe and Gerry Baker, Willie and his brother Bert were internationals for different countries – his brother representing New Zealand after emigrating there.

He made his final appearance in a Fairs Cup semi-final at Roma in a 3–3 draw and had scored his final Hibs goal against Peebles Rovers when they beat them 15–1 – the same day as Joe Baker scored 9.

After leaving, Ormond went on to play for Falkirk for a single season before becoming trainer at Brockville. He then went on to manage St Johnstone, Scotland, Hearts and Hibs for a short time.

As a Hibs player Willie Ormond won three league titles. He played 506 times, scoring 189 goals. He scored 10 or more goals in a season ten times. As manager he was in charge for 31 games, winning 14, drawing 8 and losing 9, setting the club en route to the First Division championship before standing down for Bertie Auld midway through the season.

He appeared 6 times for Scotland, scoring twice including a goal against England in a 4–2 defeat at Hampden. Two of his appearances were in Scotland's disastrous 1954 World Cup campaign. As Scotland manager, he was in charge for 38 games in the early 1970s, winning 18, drawing 8 and losing 12. He led Scotland to the World Cup in 1974, where his side were terribly unfortunate to go out at the group stages unbeaten after drawing with Brazil and Yugoslavia.

Willie was awarded the OBE in 1975, and died in 1984. He is a member of both the Hibs Hall of Fame and the Scottish Football Hall of Fame.

BROTHERS

Several sets of brothers have played for Hibs and these include:

Allan and Mark Dempsie
Greg and Graeme Miller
Alex and Jim Scott
Joe and Gerry Baker

None of these sets of brothers played together for Hibs though, despite some of them being at the club at the same time. The last set of brothers to play for Hibs were the Lauders – Tom and William – who played together 6 times in 1930.

SCORED ON THEIR DEBUTS

Many Hibs players have scored on their debut, here are some of the more interesting ones.

Brian Kerr scored less than 3 minutes into his debut against Hearts at Tynecastle. Hibs went on to record a 1–0 victory and enjoyed a superb start to the season. Sadly it wasn't to last and Kerr never scored for Hibs again, and left having played just 31 games.

Other players to score on their debut against the Edinburgh rivals were Keith Houchen in April 1989, who scored to give

Hibs the lead at Tynecastle. His time at Hibs was unhappy as the club was beset with financial problems and he left barely two years later for Port Vale having scored just 17 goals in 66 games.

Andy Dow scored on his debut at Tynecastle in March 1996 in a game that ended 1–1. He left for Aberdeen when Hibs were relegated in 1998, and came back to haunt us when he scored one of the Aberdeen goals in the Scottish Cup semi-final of 2000 when Aberdeen won 2–1.

Marc Libbra came on loan from Toulouse and scored on his debut after coming on as sub at Parkhead in a 1–1 draw in February 2001.

Stuart Beedie scored on his debut against Rangers at Easter Road in 1986 in Souness' first game as Gers boss. Beedie played just 12 games scoring 3 goals before he moved on to Dunfermline.

Out of the Famous Five, Gordon Smith, Eddie Turnbull and Willie Ormond all scored on their debuts, while Lawrie Reilly and Bobby Johnstone didn't. Joe Baker didn't either.

UNCHANGED SIDE

Hibs played 10 games in a row with the same side from when they faced East Fife in November 1949 to when they faced Stirling Albion in January 1950. The stability clearly benefitted the side, as they recorded nine wins and a draw.

The team that was used was: Tommy Younger, Davie Shaw, Jimmy Cairns, Bobby Combe, Jock Paterson, Archie Buchanan, Gordon Smith, Bobby Johnstone, Lawrie Reilly, Eddie Turnbull, Willie Ormond. The run ended when Peter Aird came in for Jock Paterson.

A couple of seasons later, Hibs played with an unchanged side for 12 consecutive games from December 1951 until February 1952. They recorded 8 wins, 2 draws and 2 losses in this period. The team this time around was: Tommy Younger,

Jock Govan, Hugh Howie, Archie Buchanan, Jock Paterson, Michael Gallacher, Gordon Smith, Bobby Johnstone, Lawrie Reilly, Eddie Turnbull, Bobby Combe. The run ended when Hibs faced Raith Rovers in the Scottish Cup at Tynecastle in a second replay. Willie Ormond returned for Eddie Turnbull, and Bobby Combe moved to inside-left. The switch and replacement didn't work out for Hibs, and they crashed to a 4–1 defeat.

NUMBERS

Hibs first wore numbered jerseys at the start of the 1946/47 season. The first game that featured this innovation was a 9–1 victory against Queen of the South. The team that day was:

1   Jimmy Kerr
2   Hugh Howie
3   Davie Shaw
4   Sammy Kean
5   Peter Aird
6   Thomas McCabe
7   Gordon Smith
8   Jock Cuthbertson
9   Jock Weir
10   Archie Buchanan
11   Johnny Aitkenhead

LOW GOALSCORER

Hugh Howie was a dependable defender who arrived at Hibs from Newton Juniors during the Second World War. He was to go on to play 268 games for the club, but only scored a solitary goal which helped Hibs win the 'longest game ever' against Motherwell in a Scottish Cup semi-final in 1947. He retired early from the game on medical advice and turned to journalism. Sadly, he was just 33 when he died in a car crash. Hugh received one Scotland cap, against Wales in 1948. It is surprising to note given his scoring record with Hibs that he scored on his Scotland debut.

CONSECUTIVE CLEAN SHEETS

Hibs kept a record 7 clean sheets in a row in January and February 1923, over 4 Scottish Cup games and 3 league games. The run finally came to an end when Hibs lost 1–0 to Morton on Valentines Day.

MOST CONSECUTIVE GAMES WITHOUT SCORING

Hibs went 7 games without scoring at the start of 2011. Paul Hanlon scored the last goal before the run with a last-minute equaliser at home to Dundee United on 29 December. The run was broken by Derek Riordan when he scored a 63rd minute strike in a 2–0 home victory over St Mirren.

MOST CONSECUTIVE GAMES WITHOUT A CLEAN SHEET

Hibs managed to go 37 games without keeping a clean sheet from February 1959 onwards. It was January 1960 before they managed to stop the opposition from scoring in a game when custodian Willie Muirhead shut out Third Lanark in a 6–0 victory.

MOST CONSECUTIVE SCORING GAMES

Hibs managed to go just over a full year scoring in every game – 48 games from 1 March 1947 until 27 March 1948 when they met Rangers in the Scottish Cup semi-final (Hibs lost the semi-final 1–0).

LONGEST LOSING STREAK

During the First World War, Hibernian often found it difficult to field a full-strength team, so it is perhaps unsurprising that this is when they had their worst losing streak. They lost 9 games on the trot from the end of March 1917 until they beat Airdrie 3–1 in September. They scored 2 goals and conceded 17 on this run.

LONGEST STREAK WITHOUT WINNING

Hibs have gone 15 games without winning on four occasions, the most recent being in 1997. After beating Dunfermline Athletic 5–2 on 13 September, Hibs failed to win another game until meeting Dunfermline again on 10 January, Stephen Crawford scoring the winner on that occasion. However, the victory disguised little as Hibs won 1 in 24 outings including that game, and it was no surprise when they were relegated at the end of the season.

MOST CONSECUTIVE DRAWS

Most Hibs fans will be unsurprised to learn that the record for consecutive draws was set under Alex Miller. Hibs drew six consecutive games after a stalemate with Kilmarnock in September 1994. Ties followed against Aberdeen, Motherwell, Celtic, Partick Thistle and Falkirk.

TOPPED THE SCORING CHART

A few Hibs players have topped the national scoring charts, and these are listed below:

David Reid	1902/03	14
Lawrie Reilly	1950/51	22
	1951/52	27
	1952/53 (shared)	30
Joe Baker	1958/59	25
	1959/60	42
Alan Gordon	1972/73	27

I DON'T FANCY THAT

In August 2011, Hibernian recruited Phil Airey on loan from Newcastle United. However, after one solitary substitute appearance in a 4–1 defeat at Kilmarnock, the Englishman decided that he in fact didn't fancy Hibs at all and returned to Newcastle with his loan ripped up.

LEGENDS – JOE BAKER

As the Famous Five came to the end of their careers, and left to go to other clubs or retired, Hibs fans certainly needed a boost as their team struggled. Lawrie Reilly had been an incredible striker for Hibs, but what followed was just as exceptional – Joe Baker.

By a quirk of fate, Joe had been born in Liverpool in 1940 and despite growing up in Lanarkshire, his birthplace was to have an impact on what happened during his career. After a short spell in the juniors, where he played alongside future Hibs and Arsenal team-mate Johnny MacLeod, he moved on to the Hibs first team where he made his debut at the tender age of 17 at Airdrie in the League Cup. Unfortunately this game was to result in a 4–1 loss. It wasn't long, however, before he established himself in the Hibs team and on his second appearance he scored both goals in a 2–0 victory over Queen's Park. His fourth game versus St Mirren was marked by a hat-trick. Later that season, he scored all 4 goals against Hearts at Tynecastle in a Scottish Cup victory (Hearts were a fine side, and won the league that season). The 17-year-old had well and truly arrived.

The goals continued, 30 the following season, and 46 the next. In the final season of his first spell at Hibs he notched another 44. People were taking notice. As he had been born in England, the rules of the time dictated that was the only country he could represent, so although he considered himself Scottish, it was never to be. He was called up to the England squad and made his debut against Northern Ireland in 1959. He was the first player to be selected for England without ever having played for a club in the English football leagues, a long time before Owen Hargreaves became the second. He was to go on to win 8 England caps, scoring 3 goals. He returned briefly to the side in 1965 and was unfortunate not to be selected for England's World Cup party in 1966.

Baker left Hibs before his 21st birthday after a disagreement over wages, and with many potential suitors he chose to go to Italy where Torino had offered him fantastic wages. The fee was £75,000 which was an enormous amount of money at the time. However, he suffered a serious car crash while in Italy and was happy to return to Arsenal after just a year. He went on to play for Nottingham Forest and Sunderland before he returned to Hibs nearly 10 years after he had first left. On his second debut he scored – naturally – as Hibs beat an in-form Aberdeen side who had gone 3 months without conceding a goal. Baker was to move on to Raith Rovers after just 18 months, where he ended his career.

In total he played 194 competitive games for Hibs, scoring 158 goals. He won a solitary runners-up medal in his time at the club, losing the 1958 Scottish Cup final to Clyde 2–0. Joe died in 2003.

BIGGEST CROWDS

27 Mar 1948	Scottish Cup semi-final	N	Rangers	1–0 L	142,070
22 Mar 1947	League Cup semi-final	N	Rangers	3–1 L	123,654
20 May 1953	Coronation Cup final	A	Celtic	2–0 L	117,000
29 Apr 1950	league	A	Rangers	0–0 D	115,000
6 May 1972	Scottish Cup final	N	Celtic	6–1 L	105,909
10 Feb 1951	Scottish Cup second round	A	Rangers	3–2 W	102,342
26 Apr 1958	Scottish Cup final	N	Clyde	1–0 L	95,123
22 Feb 1947	Scottish Cup third round	A	Rangers	0–0 D	95,000
19 Apr 1947	Scottish Cup final	N	Aberdeen	2–1 L	80,640
31 Mar 1923	Scottish Cup final	N	Celtic	1–0 L	80,100

SCOTTISH CUP FINAL 2012

Most Hibs fans have successfully wiped this from memory, after the dreadful events of the day. Nevertheless there's a couple of things that are worthy of mention. This was the fourth best-attended Hibs v Hearts game of all time, after the Easter Road derbies of 1950, 1956 and 1960.

It's obviously well known that Hibs haven't enjoyed the best of luck in the Scottish Cup, but it became apparent that this time around they had been drawn as the 'home' team. This turned into something that might prove significant, as it transpired that on the seven occasions they had been drawn as the 'away' team they lost on each occasion. Sadly, this wasn't to prove significant and they crashed 5–1.

COMPLETE LEAGUE RECORD

In 119 seasons of league football, this is Hibernian's complete record:

	P	W	D	L	F	A
Home	1,926	965	443	518	3,718	2,401
Away	1,924	567	437	920	2,589	3,350
Total	3,850	1,532	880	1,438	6,307	5,751

LOWEST CROWDS

28 Apr 1934	league	A	Dundee	1–0 L	350
8 Jul 2006	Intertoto	A	Dinaburg	3–0 W	350
19 Aug 1893	league	A	Thistle	2–1 W	500
7 Apr 1894	league	H	Northern	6–0 W	500
22 Dec 1894	league	H	Cowlairs	8–2 W	500
28 Mar 1925	league	A	Morton	2–2 D	500
16 Dec 1899	league	H	Third Lanark	3–2 W	700
23 Dec 1899	league	H	Clyde	5–0 W	700
30 Nov 1983	League Cup	A	Airdrie	3–1 W	738
27 August 1983	League Cup	A	Dumbarton	2–1 W	760

BIGGEST HOME CROWDS

2 Jan 1950	league	Hearts	2–1 L	65,840
2 Jan 1956	league	Hearts	2–2 D	60,812
17 Jan 1953	league	Rangers	1–1 D	60,500
3 Nov 1951	league	Rangers	1–1 D	55,000
1 Jan 1960	league	Hearts	5–1 L	54,000
2 Oct 1948	League Cup	Celtic	4–2 W	53,000
31 Jan 1948	league	Rangers	1–0 W	52,750
30 Aug 1952	League Cup	Celtic	3–0 W	52,000
5 Nov 1949	league	Rangers	1–0 W	51,500
19 Feb 1949	league	Rangers	1–0 L	50,000

SMALLEST HOME CROWDS

22 Dec 1894	league	Cowlairs	8–2 W	500
7 Apr 1894	league	Northern	6–0 W	500
23 Dec 1899	league	Clyde	5–0 W	700
16 Dec 1899	league	Third Lanark	3–2 W	700
23 Mar 1955	league	Stirling Albion	4–1 W	875
11 Mar 1931	league	Queen's Park	4–2 W	1,000
22 Nov 1930	league	Kilmarnock	3–2 W	1,000
26 Apr 1930	league	Morton	1–0 L	1,000
14 Oct 1916	league	Ayr United	4–1 L	1,000
30 May 1910	league	Hamilton Acad	1–0 W	1,000
23 May 1910	league	Motherwell	1–0 W	1,000
4 May 1907	league	Hamilton Acad	1–0 L	1,000
17 Dec 1898	league	Clyde	2–1 W	1,000
5 Sep 1896	league	Rangers	4–3 W	1,000
2 Feb 1895	league	Motherwell	5–0 W	1,000
3 Nov 1894	league	Abercorn	4–2 W	1,000
4 Nov 1893	league	Thistle	4–0 W	1,000
7 Oct 1893	league	Cowlairs	4–3 L	1,000
26 August 1893	league	Morton	9–2 W	1,000
5 May 1980	league	Partick Thistle	1–0 L	1,191

THEY DIED AT THEIR DESKS

Dan McMichael was Hibernian's first manager, and was in charge for two periods ranging from 1901–3 and 1904–19. Irish-born, he had no prior playing connections with Hibernian, but he was the brother-in-law of Hibs player James 'Judge' Murphy. All told he was in charge for 598 games, of which Hibs won 218, drew 134 and lost 246. His first game in charge was against Hearts at Tynecastle which Hibs lost 2–1. His final game in charge was away to Falkirk on 1 February 1919 just a few days before his death. Dan died on 6 February 1919 due to heart failure caused by chronic bronchitis, a victim of the Spanish 'Flu epidemic.

Willie McCartney had been Hearts manager before arriving at Easter Road in 1936. His tenure was interrupted by the Second World War, but his post-war Hibs side was exciting and on the verge of great things. Sadly, he would not see it, as he collapsed at Cliftonhill in January 1948 just a few short months before Hibernian clinched the title. All told McCartney was in charge for 484 games, of which Hibs won 241, drew 91 and lost 152. His first game in charge was a 3–1 home defeat against Aberdeen.

CHAMPIONS VIII – 1980/81

The late 1970s had seen a dreadful decline in Hibernian's fortunes, as the best players were sold on and their replacements were not up to the previous standard. Hibs managed to get to the Scottish Cup final in 1979, and came very close to winning the trophy, but it only covered the cracks and Hibs were relegated the following season. Not even an ageing George Best could save them.

It quickly became clear, however, that Hibs were too good for this division, and despite an opening day setback at home to Raith Rovers there was never any real doubt that Hibs would bounce straight back up to the Scottish top flight. Players of the calibre of Peter Cormack returned, and along with the survivors of Turnbull's Tornadoes they formed a formidable unit conceding just 22 goals.

Hibs clinched the title when they won at home to Raith Rovers in the second last game. Willie Ormond, who had taken over from his Famous Five team-mate Eddie Turnbull only remained in post for the opening few games of the campaign, before he passed on the reins to Partick Thistle manager Bertie Auld. Although Bertie was a former player, it's fair to say that Hibs fans never really took to his style of football.

	P	W	D	L	F	A	Pts
Hibernian	39	25	8	6	67	22	58
Dundee	39	22	8	9	64	40	52
St Johnstone	39	21	10	8	64	44	52
Raith Rovers	39	20	10	9	49	32	50
Motherwell	39	19	11	9	65	51	49
Ayr United	39	17	11	11	59	42	45
Hamilton Academicals	39	15	7	17	61	57	37
Dumbarton	39	13	11	15	49	50	37
Falkirk	39	13	8	18	39	52	34
Clydebank	39	10	13	16	48	59	33
East Stirlingshire	39	6	16	17	39	57	28
Dunfermline Athletic	39	10	7	22	41	58	27
Stirling Albion	39	6	11	22	19	48	23
Berwick Rangers	39	5	11	23	30	82	21

9 Aug	H	Raith Rovers	1–0 L
16 Aug	A	Stirling Albion	2–0 W
23 Aug	H	Berwick Rangers	3–0 W
6 Sep	H	Motherwell	1–0 W
9 Sep	A	Dundee	2–1 W
13 Sep	A	Ayr United	3–1 W

17 Sep	H	East Stirlingshire	2–2 D
20 Sep	A	Hamilton Academical	1–1 D
27 Sep	H	Clydebank	4–1 W
1 Oct	A	Dumbarton	2–0 L
4 Oct	A	Dunfermline Athletic	2–0 W
11 Oct	H	Falkirk	2–0 W
18 Oct	A	St Johnstone	2–1 W
25 Oct	H	Ayr United	1–0 W
1 Nov	A	Motherwell	2–0 L
8 Nov	A	East Stirlingshire	1–1 D
15 Nov	H	Hamilton Academical	3–3 D
22 Nov	A	Clydebank	1–1 D
29 Nov	H	Dunfermline Athletic	1–0 W
6 Dec	A	Falkirk	2–0 W
13 Dec	H	St Johnstone	4–0 W
20 Dec	A	Dundee	1–0 L
27 Dec	H	Stirling Albion	3–0 W
1 Jan	A	Berwick Rangers	2–0 W
3 Jan	H	Dumbarton	1–0 W
10 Jan	A	Raith Rovers	2–0 L
17 Jan	H	Falkirk	1–0 W
31 Jan	A	Berwick Rangers	0–0 D
7 Feb	H	Dundee	0–0 D
21 Feb	H	Hamilton Academical	4–0 W
28 Feb	A	Dunfermline Athletic	5–0 W
18 Mar	H	St Johnstone	2–1 L
21 Mar	A	Dumbarton	4–1 W
28 Mar	A	Ayr United	1–0 W
4 Apr	H	Stirling Albion	0–0 D
11 Apr	H	East Stirlingshire	2–0 W
15 Apr	H	Clydebank	3–0 W
18 Apr	H	Raith Rovers	2–0 W
25 Apr	A	Motherwell	1–1 D

Appearances

Arthur Duncan	39
Craig Paterson	38
Ralph Callachan	38
Jim McArthur	37
Jackie McNamara	36
Gordon Rae	34
John Connolly	29 + 3
Jim Brown	29 + 2
Ally MacLeod	27 + 3
Willie Jamieson	19 + 9
Billy McLaren	18
J.A. Brown	14 +1
Gary Murray	15
Alan Sneddon	14
Paul McGlinchey	8 + 1
Ally Brazil	5 + 2
Hugh Hamill	6 + 1
Derek Rodier	1 + 6
Terry Wilson	4 + 3
Peter Cormack	3 + 3
George Best	4
George Stewart	2
Willie Murray	1 + 1
Bobby Torrance	2
Ian Black	2
Colin Kelly	2
Brian Rice	0 + 1
Stephen Brown	1
Gordon Byrne	0 + 1
Iain Hendry	1

Goals

Ally MacLeod	15
Gordon Rae	13
Willie Jamieson	12

John Connolly	8
Gary Murray	5
Ralph Callachan	4
Craig Paterson	3
Arthur Duncan	1
Jackie McNamara	1
Jim Brown	1
Ally Brazil	1
Terry Wilson	1
Peter Cormack	1

THEY SAID IT

'You build from the back. The ball is round because it is meant to roll, not fly through the air.'

John Collins

LEGENDS – EDDIE TURNBULL

Eddie arrived at Easter Road as a 23-year-old, and if his career had been affected by the war, he quickly made up for lost time. Scoring on his debut against Third Lanark, he was to make the inside-left position his own, before dropping further back to half-back later in his career. He played in the 1947 Cup final, and again in 1958 against Clyde.

Eddie went on to to be a fine manager, starting at Queen's Park in 1963 before moving on to Aberdeen where he won the Scottish Cup which had eluded him as player at Hibernian. He rejoined Hibernian as manager in 1971, where he was to stay until 1980. His 'Tornadoes' were the finest side assembled by Hibs since the Famous Five and won the League Cup in 1972, along with the Drybrough Cup in 1972 and 1973. Hibs also came the closest to winning the Scottish Cup – losing the 1979 final after 3 games to Rangers.

Eddie won his first cap at 82, thanks to journalist and sports presenter Gary Imlach whose father was in a similar position to Eddie – neither had won caps during their playing career as at that time caps were only awarded for internationals against the home nations, and Eddie never featured against Northern Ireland, Wales or England in his 9 international appearances.

Turnbull died in April 2011 at the age of 88, and Hibs' next game at home to Aberdeen was chosen as a celebration of his life. As a player he played 487 times for Hibernian, scoring 202 goals. As manager he oversaw 454 games with 219 wins, 100 draws and 125 losses. He is a member of the Hibs Hall of Fame and the Scottish Football Hall of Fame.

THE ONE THAT GOT AWAY

Alex Miller was Hibs manager when he identified a young midfielder at Crewe who he thought could be a good signing for the club. He agreed a fee, but Crewe then demanded more money and Miller was unconvinced that the player was worth it. David Platt would soon move on to Aston Villa before moving on to Serie A. He was to go on to become a full England international soon afterwards, starring in the 1990 World Cup in Italy.

A GOAL A GAME

Joe Baker managed 96 goals in 96 games at Easter Road for a perfect goal-a-game record. Closest to him were Neil Martin who managed 54 in 55 starts and Joe McBride who made 38 goals in 43 games.

UNDER-21s

Hibs have provided players for the Scottish Under-21 side from their very first European Championship game in 1976 v Czechoslovakia. Lindsay Muir made an appearance as sub, while former club-mate Pat Stanton started. Pat was by this time a Celtic player and 32 years old. 32 years old? Back in the day teams were able to field over-age players, similar to the modern-day rules for the Olympics. Also in the side for the first outing were veteran Aberdeen goalkeeper Bobby Clark, former Scotland manager George Burley, Roy Aitken and Tommy Burns of Celtic, the late Davie Cooper and David Narey and Paul Sturrock of Dundee United. Scotland drew 0–0, and failed to qualify from the group stages, losing out to Czechoslovakia on goal difference.

BIGGEST HOME WINS

11 Feb 1961	Scottish Cup	Peebles Rovers	15–1
6 Nov 1965	league	Hamilton	11–1
26 Oct 1889	Scottish Cup	Dunfermline	11–1
22 Sept 1965	League Cup	Alloa	11–2
19 May 1894	league	Port Glasgow	10–1
6 Oct 1883	Scottish Cup	Edina	10–1
23 Sep 2003	League Cup	Montrose	9–0
21 Nov 1896	league	Abercorn	9–0
12 Sep 1885	Scottish Cup	Edina	9–0
7 Dec 1878	Scottish Cup	Rob Roy	9–0

AVERAGE ATTENDANCES

The highest average attendance for Hibernian league games in a season was in the championship year of 1951/52 when they averaged a whopping 31,567. In recent times the 2006/07 average of 14,488 was last bettered in 1972/73 when it was 16,100. Since the Second World War, the lowest average was the 4,460 that followed the team in the old First Division season of 1980/81 when Hibs were champions.

BIGGEST AWAY WINS

24 Oct 1959	league		Airdrie	11–1
9 Jan 1897	Scottish Cup		Duncrab Park	10–1
19 Dec 1959	league		Partick Thistle	10–2
25 Jan 1947	Scottish Cup		Alloa	8–0
31 Mar 1945	Southern League Cup		Albion Rovers	8–1
10 Nov 1883	Scottish Cup		5th KRV	8–1
1 Jan 1973	league		Hearts	7–0
29 Aug 1896	league		Clyde	7–0

BIGGEST LOSSES

30 Dec 1995	league	A	Rangers	7–0
29 Mar 1935	league	A	Airdrie	7–0
15 Nov 1930	league	A	Aberdeen	7–0
6 Dec 1919	league	A	Rangers	7–0
15 Feb 1919	league	A	Morton	9–2
24 Dec 1898	league	A	Rangers	10–0
27 Sep 1890	Scottish Cup	H	Dumbarton	9–1

LEGENDS – HARRY SWAN

Harry Swan was a master baker by trade, and was Hibernian chairman through the most successful period of their history. Originally a Leith Athletic fan, he first came to prominence at Easter Road as debenture holder in 1924 when funds were required for the building of a new grandstand. He was first elected to the board in 1931, but resigned less than a year later when the team failed to gain promotion and accused his fellow directors of lacking ambition and of being overly cautious with funds.

In 1934, Swan was again nominated for election to the board by the body of debenture holders and was duly welcomed for a second time. To his surprise Owen Brannigan stood down and he was elected chairman – he was 38 years old at the time.

Swan's ambition was to make Hibs great again within 10 years, and if one takes account of the war then he was successful in his aim. He was an excellent administrator, and was behind many significant changes to Scottish football at this time.

After 29 years at the helm, Swan sold Hibernian to William Harrower in the summer of 1963. He remained as a director until shortly before his death in 1966. After his death a plaque dedicated to his memory was unveiled in the boardroom by the then directors of the club. Swan's daughter Betty recently dedicated the plaque in the new board of the West Stand at Easter Road in a ceremony attended by all current directors.

WE'RE GOING TO WIN 6–5

On 17 September 1966 Hibs visited Dunfermline in the league, and in a tense match emerged victors 6–5. The Hibernian team that day was: Thomson Allan, Bobby Duncan, Joe Davis, Pat Stanton, John McNamee, Alan Cousin, Peter Cormack, Colin Stein, Jim Scott, Allan McGraw and Eric Stevenson. In front of 9,312 the goals were scored by Peter Cormack, Eric Stevenson and doubles from Jim Scott and Alan McGraw.

Hibernian have also been on the wrong end of a couple of 6–5 defeats, curiously just months apart. In the Southern League in 1940 Hibs lost at Easter Road to Hearts in January, and then again to Falkirk in May. The Hearts game was played in a heavy fog which meant many of the crowd were unsure as to what was going on.

TWELVE-GOAL THRILLER

Hibs have twice been victors by an 8–4 scoreline. In December 1925 Hibernian beat Hamilton 8–4, and on Christmas Eve 1960 they beat Third Lanark by the same scoreline.

HIGH SCORING DRAWS

Hibernian have twice been involved in 5–5 draws, firstly against St Mirren in February 1958. In front of 12,000 at Easter Road, Eddie Turnbull, Jim Thomson, Joe Baker and Willie Ormond were the scorers.

Less than two years later, they were involved in another one, this time against Clyde. The scorers on this occasion were Joe Baker who scored a hat-trick, and Bobby Johnstone who scored a double.

YOUNGEST CAPS

Willie Groves is Hibs' youngest capped player – he made his debut against Wales in the British Home Championship on 10 March 1888 aged just 18 years 122 days. He marked the occasion with a goal in a 5–1 win but was to receive just 2 further caps as a Celtic player.

Garry O'Connor is Hibernian's youngest full cap in the twenty-first century making his debut against Nigeria on 17 April 2002 in a 2–1 home defeat.

TOP OF THE POPS

Peter Marinello was still a teenager when he moved to Arsenal from Hibs, and his good looks did not go unnoticed by a media desperate for more George Best-type football players. Subsequently he appeared as a guest presenter on *Top of the Pops*.

HANDS OFF HIBS

When Wallace Mercer tried to take over Hibernian in 1990 and merge them with Hearts, a protest group called Hands off Hibs was born. John Leslie just happened to be the presenter of children's TV show *Blue Peter*, and he used the opportunity to appear on the programme wearing a Hands off Hibs t-shirt.

OH COME ON REF!

Hibs should have known that it wasn't to be their year when Craig Thomson was appointed referee for the Scottish Cup final of 2012. The ref had previously been in charge in six games that season, and Hibs had lost them all without scoring a goal. To make matters worse, he had awarded Aberdeen a game-winning penalty when it was clearly a dive. While reffing Hearts, the cup final rivals, he had overseen four wins and a draw in the same season. To make matters even worse, he had awarded five penalties against Hibs in the previous two seasons and hadn't awarded any in their favour.

It didn't come as much of a surprise then, when in the final itself he failed to show Hearts' Ian Black a red card in the opening minutes then awarded a penalty and sent off Pa Saikou Kujabi early in the second half, ending the game as a contest.

CHAMPIONS IX – 1998/99

The catastrophic reign of Jim Duffy had left Hibs in a perilous state, and although Alex McLeish's side fought valiantly they were relegated from the SPL after a home defeat by Dundee United in May 1998.

Despite a shaky start with a home loss against Stranraer in the first ever league meeting between the sides, and a loss at Paisley, Hibs soon settled into their stride and were top of the league and clear by the Christmas holidays when some bumper crowds turned up to see Hibernian against Ayr United and their closest rivals Falkirk.

Hibs were bolstered by an incredible run of 13 successive victories, and indeed they won 20 of their final 21 league games. This season saw Hibs gain some excellent players and Mixu Paatelainen, Russell Latapy and Franck Sauzée all signed on after careers that had seen them star for their countries.

Hibs clinched the title against Hamilton on 3 April with five games remaining, marking their return to the SPL.

	P	W	D	L	F	A	Pts
Hibernian	36	28	5	3	84	33	89
Falkirk	36	20	6	10	60	38	66
Ayr United	36	19	5	12	66	42	62
Airdrie	36	18	5	13	42	43	59
St Mirren	36	14	10	12	42	43	52
Morton	36	14	7	15	45	41	49
Clydebank	36	11	13	12	36	38	46
Raith Rovers	36	8	11	17	37	57	35
Hamilton Academical	36	6	10	20	30	62	28
Stranraer	36	5	2	29	29	74	17

4 Aug	A	Morton	1–0 W
15 Aug	H	Stranraer	2–1 L

22 Aug	A	Falkirk	1–1 D
29 Aug	H	Ayr United	4–2 W
5 Sep	A	Clydebank	2–2 D
12 Sep	A	St Mirren	2–0 L
19 Sep	H	Raith Rovers	3–1 W
26 Sep	H	Hamilton Academical	0–0 D
3 Oct	A	Airdrieonians	3–1 W
10 Oct	A	Stranraer	1–0 W
17 Oct	H	Morton	2–1 W
24 Oct	A	Ayr United	3–3 D
31 Oct	H	Clydebank	2–1 W
7 Nov	A	Raith Rovers	3–1 W
21 Nov	A	Hamilton Academical	2–2 D
24 Nov	H	St Mirren	4–1 W
28 Nov	H	Airdrieonians	1–0 W
5 Dec	A	Morton	3–1 W
12 Dec	H	Falkirk	2–1 W
19 Dec	H	Clydebank	3–0 W
26 Dec	H	Ayr United	3–0 W
2 Jan	H	Raith Rovers	5–1 W
9 Jan	A	St Mirren	2–1 W
16 Jan	H	Hamilton Academical	4–0 W
30 Jan	A	Airdrieonians	4–1 W
6 Feb	H	Stranraer	2–0 W
20 Feb	A	Falkirk	2–1 W
27 Feb	A	Ayr United	3–1 W
13 Mar	A	Clydebank	2–0 L
20 Mar	H	Airdrieonians	3–0 W
3 Apr	A	Hamilton Academical	2–0 W
10 Apr	A	Raith Rovers	3–1 W
17 Apr	H	St Mirren	2–1 W
24 Apr	H	Morton	2–1 W
1 May	A	Stranraer	4–0 W
8 May	H	Falkirk	2–1 W

Appearances

Ole Gottskálksson	36
Stevie Crawford	28 + 7
Shaun Dennis	29 + 2
Stuart Lovell	26 + 5
Pat McGinlay	29 + 1
Barry Lavety	9 + 18
Mixu Paatelainen	25 + 1
Justin Skinner	24
John Hughes	22 + 1
Russell Latapy	23
Paul Holsgrove	9 + 9
Paul Lovering	17
Michael Renwick	15 + 1
Derek Collins	16
Tony Rougier	10 + 5
Barry Prenderville	13
Paul Hartley	6 + 7
Scott Bannerman	2 + 10
Alex Marinkov	10
Franck Sauzée	9
David Elliot	8
Peter Guggi	7 + 1
Mark Dempsie	5 + 3
Kenny Miller	5 + 2
Derek Anderson	6
Tom Smith	3 + 2
Eric Paton	1 + 3
Kevin Harper	0 + 2
Rab Shannon	1
Paul Tosh	1
Klaus Dietrich	1
Alan Reid	0 + 1
Emilio Bottiglieri	0 + 1
Tom McManus	0 + 1

Goals

Stevie Crawford	14
Pat McGinlay	12
Mixu Paatelainen	12
Stuart Lovell	11
Russell Latapy	6
Paul Hartley	5
Shaun Dennis	3
John Hughes	3
Barry Lavety	2
Justin Skinner	2
Barry Prenderville	2
Franck Sauzée	2
Peter Guggi	2
Paul Holsgrove	1
Paul Lovering	1
Tony Rougier	1
Alex Marinkov	1
Kenny Miller	1
Kevin Harper	1

AWAY GOALS

The away goals rule was introduced in European football in the mid-1960s as a tiebreaker if teams finished level. In common with most Scottish teams, the rule has not been kind to Hibernian and they have lost every time it has been applied.

In January 1969, Hibernian were drawn against then West German side SV Hamburg. Hibs were unfortunate to lose the first leg 1–0 away, and were even more unfortunate to only win the second leg 2–1 ensuring they would exit the Fairs Cup with the relatively newfangled rule that away goals counted double in the event of the teams finishing level. Hibs could have easily qualified, but were undone by two disallowed first half goals at Easter Road, along with an uncharacteristic penalty miss by the normally reliable Joe Davis. A blunder by Bobby Duncan allowed West German international Uwe Seeler to score for the visitors, which left Hibs victors on the night, but out the tournament.

After winning the Skol Cup in 1991, Hibernian entered the 1992/93 UEFA Cup where they were somewhat unfortunate to draw Belgian side Anderlecht in the first round whose line up included many international players. In the first leg at home, Hibs gave an exceptional account of themselves, and took an early lead through Dave Beaumont. However, by midway through the second half they found themselves 2–1 down following a soft penalty being conceded and scored by Marc Degryse, and a strike from Peter Van Vossen, who was later to play for Rangers. Things went from bad to worse for Hibs, and Mickey Weir was unjustly sent off with just 16 minutes remaining. Hibs rallied at this though, and were deserving of the equaliser through Pat McGinlay in the closing minutes.

Nobody gave them much of a chance in Belgium in the return leg, and an early goal from Luc Nilis seemed to confirm this: Hibs rallied though, and were back on level terms inside 15 minutes when Darren Jackson equalised. These were to be the only goals of the game, and Hibs departed the competition unbeaten in the opening round.

In 2006, Hibernian entered the Intertoto Cup, which was both a means to get some games under their belt pre-season, but also could lead to a lucrative UEFA Cup place. Hibs received a bye in the first round, and eliminated Latvian side FC Dinaburg in some style, winning 8–0 on aggregate. In the third round was a much sterner test – they were drawn to play Danish side Odense BK. The winners of this game would advance to a qualifier for the group stages of the UEFA Cup, and Hibs would make acquaintance with an old adversary, and a former Hibs player. Odense were managed at this time by Bruce Rioch who had been captain of the Derby County side who had played Hibs in a friendly game to celebrate Hibs' centenary in 1975. Ulrik Laursen, on the other hand, had played for Hibs at the turn of the millennium and had been a cultured wing-back and accomplished central defender who had moved on to Celtic after leaving Easter Road, before returning to his homeland where he had won international caps for Denmark.

Hibs were drawn in Denmark in the first leg, and a cagey game was decided by a solitary goal from the penalty spot for the home side. Hibernian fancied their chances in the return, but the 10,641 crowd was left flat when the first goal of the game went to Odense early in the second half, leaving the hosts requiring three goals to advance. Undeterred, Hibs quickly equalised through Rob Jones, before taking the lead on the day through Paul Dalglish with just 11 minutes remaining. Hibs threw everything at their rivals, utilising 6ft 7in central defender Rob Jones as an auxiliary forward – but it was to no avail and they departed the competition on away goals yet again.

In addition to the games mentioned above, Hibs also played in two ties which finished level after two games. Both these were before the away goals rule was introduced and they both went to a third, play-off game. Hibernian unfortunately lost both.

In April 1961 Hibs faced Italian side Roma for a place in the Fairs Cup final. The first leg at home was a 2–2 draw, Joe Baker and Johnny MacLeod scoring for Hibs. The return match a week later in Italy was also a draw, this time 3–3, Joe Baker netting with a double, with Bobby Kinloch also scoring. The more astute readers will realise that under the present-day rules Hibs would have qualified for the third Fairs Cup final, but the rules of the time dictated that it should be a play-off and Roma won the right to stage it. The play-off took place at the end of May, and for Hibs this was their first competitive game for four weeks. The lack of match practice showed and they were heavily defeated 6–0. This was to be the last game for Joe Baker and Johnny MacLeod who both moved on for big transfer fees in the close season. Roma went on to defeat English side Birmingham City in a two-legged final. Future Hibs player and manager Bertie Auld featured for the losing side.

In September 1965, Hibernian beat Spanish side Valencia 2–0 at Easter Road in a first round Fairs Cup tie; John McNamee and Jim Scott were the scorers. Five weeks later, Hibs ventured to Spain and this game produced an identical scoreline but this this time in favour of the Spanish side. The rules of the time meant that a play-off was necessary, and Hibs were unlucky to have to return to Spain for a one-off game. They did so in November 1965 and were unfortunate to lose 3–0. An early goal for the Spaniards by Munoz was all that separated the sides going into the final quarter, and Hibs had created a number of good chances which their forwards did not manage to convert. Unfortunately another goal did come for the Spaniards, ending the tie before they added another to progress to the next round with a 3–0 victory.

THEY SAID IT

'It's not a question of any sum of money in return for that integrity – integrity is beyond purchase.'

Rod Petrie

CUP WINNERS I – SCOTTISH CUP 1886/87

Hibs announced their arrival at the national level with a stunning victory over Dumbarton. Hibs had made the semi-final four years in a row, but finally made it past that stage in 1887 and won the final at their first attempt.

The semi-final victory over Vale was marred by allegations of professionalism, which Hibs were cleared of. Hibs went a goal behind, but goals from Montgomery and Groves secured the cup.

First round

11 Sep	H	Durhamstown Rangers	6–1 W

Second round

2 Oct	A	Mossend Swifts	1–1 D
9 Oct	H	Mossend Swifts	3–0 W

Third round

23 Oct	H	Hearts	5–1 W

Fourth round

4 Dec	H	Queen of the South Wanderers	7–3 W

Quarter-final

25 Dec	A	Third Lanark	2–1 W

Semi-final

22 Jan	H	Vale of Leven	3–1 W

Final

12 Feb	N	Dumbarton	2–1 W*

*At Second Hampden, attendance 15,000.

Goalscorers: Willie Groves, James Montgomery

Team

John Tobin, James Lundy, Barney Fagan, James McGhee, Peter McGinn, James McLaren, James Montgomery, Willie Groves, Paddy Lafferty, George Smith, Phil Clarke

Appearances

John Tobin	8
James Lundy	8
Barney Fagan	8
James McGhee	8
Peter McGinn	8
James McLaren	8
Willie Groves	8
George Smith	8
Phil Clarke	8
Jerry Reynolds	7
Pat McGovern	2
James Montgomery	2
Paddy O'Donnell	1
Tommy Lee	1
Paddy Hannan	1
Tom Maley	1
Paddy Lafferty	1

Goals

Willie Groves	10
Jerry Reynolds	4
Phil Clarke	4
James McGhee	3
George Smith	3
James Montgomery	2
Peter McGinn	1
James McLaren	1
Untraced	1

EUROPEAN TIES

Hibs have been involved in three European ties, which have each finished all-square after the second leg with an identical scoreline as the first leg. These ties have all finished in the same way – with defeat for Hibs.

The first of these games was back in 1973 when Hibs faced Leeds United in the Fairs Cup second round. The first leg at Elland Road finished goalless, and the return leg ended the same way. Unsurprisingly, an extra 30 minutes did not manage to separate the sides as Leeds withstood immense Hibs pressure, resulting in the game going to a penalty shoot-out. Pat Stanton hit the post with the first penalty, and he was the only player to miss as Leeds moved into the next round winning 5–4 on penalties. This Leeds side went on to win the English league championship at the end of the season.

In 1989 Hibs faced RFC Liège in the UEFA Cup second round, after disposing of Hungarian side Videoton in the first round with a particularly impressive victory in the away leg. Again, both legs in this tie finished goalless, and Hibs would have cause to rue the penalty miss by Keith Houchen in the first leg at Easter Road. The second leg was 10 minutes into injury time when Jean-François De Sart hit a speculative long-range shot, which Andy Goram was unable to keep out. Hibs were unable to conjure up the goal required to level things on the night, and again Hibs went out. Danny Boffin featured for Liège in this game, and he was to play against Hibs again, this time for Anderlecht when they met a couple of years later.

In 2001, Hibernian again qualified for the UEFA Cup, and this time they came up against Greek opposition for the first time. AEK Athens had previously played in the Champions League so nobody underestimated the huge task Hibs had before them in their first European venture in nine years, and yet they were to come so close.

The first leg in Athens was postponed for a week after the 11 September terror atrocity in the United States. Many Hibs fans therefore missed the match, although a good number stayed out for an extra week's holiday. When the game did come around, Hibs struggled against the Greeks and in particular they missed talisman and rock Franck Sauzée who was out injured. They did manage to go in level at half time, but a second-half penalty from Tsartas and a header from Demis Nikolaidis gave Hibernian a tough task in the second leg at Easter Road. Back in Edinburgh a week later the ground was packed and noisy, and Hibs were able to call on Franck Sauzée and Craig Brewster again. Hibs attacked the visitors relentlessly down the flanks with de la Cruz causing particular problems. Again, just as a week previously the game was even at half time, but continued Hibs pressure led to Spaniard Paco Luna opening the scoring early in the second half. Hibs then drew level on aggregate with just 9 minutes remaining when Paco got on the end of an Ulrik Laursen cross. In the final minute Paco had the chance of a hat-trick, and to seal a famous victory, but his header went just the wrong side of the post.

The match moved into extra time, where the inevitable happened – Tsartas scored with a fine strike, before adding another when he flicked home from a corner. This left Hibs the impossible task of scoring another three goals to qualify. David Zitelli rounded off the scoring with an exquisite 30-yard strike, leaving Hibernian victors on the night, but out of Europe once more.

AEK were an excellent side though, and it was only perhaps when Greece won the 2004 European Championship that many appreciated just what a fine performance Hibs had put up. Theodoros Zagorakis captained the Greeks to glory, along with Vassilios Tsartas, Demis Nikolaidis, Michalis Kapsis and Vassilis Lakis. All had featured against Hibs.

LEGENDS – WILLIE McCARTNEY

McCartney had been manager of Hearts for 15 years before taking over at Hibs in 1936. He had been approached to take over from temporary manager Johnny Halligan but initially refused – instead waiting to see if Hibs were saved from relegation, before committing to take the job. Halligan duly saw them to safety and he became manager a year after leaving Hearts. Initially Hibs struggled under his charge, winning just two home games in his first season but things slowly improved and the manager was able to attract a better standard of player to Easter Road. Trophies started to come during the war too; Hibs won the Summer Cup in 1941 and then the Southern League Cup followed in 1944.

They would go on to to win the league in 1948, but alas McCartney was not to witness the fruits of his labours after he took ill at a Scottish Cup tie against Albion Rovers in January 1948. Manager McCartney complained of feeling unwell towards the end of the game, and he was accompanied home by Wilson Terris, a long-time director of the club, and Eddie Turnbull. McCartney later died from a massive coronary.

McCartney had an excellent record against Hearts and the Old Firm. He managed Hibs in 484 games, winning 241 of them, drawing 91 and losing 152. In the process they scored 1,104 goals.

GIANT KILLING

As one of the bigger clubs in Scottish football Hibernian have always been vulnerable to shock results against the so-called minnows of the game. Three of the worst ever are as follows.

The First World War had been a wretched time for Hibs and the seasons afterwards were tough. In 1919/20 they finished 18th out of 22 teams, and crashed out of the Scottish Cup at non-league Armadale. The result was not entirely unexpected; Hibs had just managed to sneak past non-league Galston (a small town near Kilmarnock) after a replay in the first round when they came up against Armadale away from home in the second. In front of a crowd of 5,000 Hibs dominated proceedings in the first half, but it was Armadale that scored. Hibs just weren't able to take advantage of all the corners and chances they were creating and the Armadale goalkeeper was in superb form. After the interval Armadale came into the game more, but it was Hibs who had the best chances, though they failed to take them. The game petered out with Hibernian on the wrong end of a 1–0 scoreline.

Another shocker was when Hibernian lost to their capital rivals Edinburgh City in 1938. This game proved that even the best managers in the land can have off days. The Hibs manager for the game was the legendary Willie McCartney who had started to mould his own team after taking over in 1936. In this first round game Hibernian were on top for large portions, but simply didn't take their chances, while the visitors, ably led by former Hibs player Peter Carruthers, took what opportunities came their way to lead 2–1 at the break. Early in the second half, City extended their lead when Carruthers scored his second and Edinburgh City's third. Hibs pulled a goal back through James Miller and were given the perfect opportunity to take the tie to a second game in the closing minutes when they were awarded a penalty. The normally reliable Arthur Milne stepped up and sent the ball against the crossbar, and in the final minutes Hibs were unable to fashion the equaliser, meaning that they exited the cup. Edinburgh City finished 17th out of 18 teams in the Old Scottish Second Division that season, winning just 7 league games out of 34. They lost all but 3 of their 17 away games, winning just once. In the second round City capitulated at Starks Park to Raith Rovers 9–2. Hibs, in contrast, finished a respectable 10th in the top league, losing just three games at Easter Road outwith the cup.

In recent times, Hibernian's worst cup performance has been when they exited the Scottish Cup in a fourth round replay defeat to Ayr United, who at the time played in the Scottish Second Division – two leagues lower than Hibs. This was a match early in Colin Calderwood's reign during a period when Hibs couldn't buy a goal. After an uninspiring goalless draw at home in the first leg, Hibs ventured down to Ayrshire for the replay. Ian Murray and Derek Riordan were the only survivors from the infamous night in 2002 when Hibs had lost to Ayr United in the League Cup semi-final at Hampden – the score that night was also 1–0 to Ayr United.

Ayr United veteran Mark Roberts scored the only goal of the game after 19 minutes, and while Hibs had threatened the visitors' goal, they ran out of steam in the second period and Ayr coasted to victory. This is the only time Ayr have ever beaten Hibs in the Scottish Cup.

FRIENDLIES

In the course of their history Hibs gained a reputation for being pioneers, especially when it came to travel and playing teams from foreign nations. In addition to the games in European competitions that Hibs have played, they have also played friendlies against – among others – Feyenoord, Bayern Munich, Marseille, Rosenborg, Torino, Vasco Da Gama and Borussia Dortmund. They have managed to beat all of those teams too, and in the case of Bayern Munich on more than one occasion.

CONSECUTIVE CUP FINALS

One of the best Hibernian teams never to win anything was the team of the mid-1920s which made successive Scottish Cup finals in 1923 and 1924. Incredible as it may seem today, Hibs fielded the same team in both years: Willie Harper, Willie McGinnigle, Willie Dornan, Peter Kerr, Willie Miller,

Hugh Shaw, Harry Ritchie, Jimmy Dunn, Jimmy McColl, Johnny Halligan and John Walker. This team was particularly unfortunate in 1923, as they only conceded a solitary goal in the whole year's competition – that being the only goal of the final against Celtic. The final itself was a dour affair, with defences holding solid for entire match and it would take a flash of brilliance or a mistake – or both – to settle the match, and this is what happened as Hibernian's goalkeeper misjudged a cross, and an awkward bounce of the ball allowed Cassidy to score for Celtic.

On paper, Hibs had an easier final in 1924 when they met Airdrie at Ibrox. The route to the final was one of the longest Hibs were ever to experience, the final being their eleventh game in that season's tournament. After safely negotiating the first round, Hibs required a reply to dispose of Alloa Athletic, before an excellent win at Ibrox put Rangers out in the third round. Thereafter, it took three games to dispose of Partick Thistle in the quarter-finals, and another three games to beat Aberdeen in the semi-finals. Unfortunately Hibs could not repeat their earlier win at Ibrox and a smooth flowing Airdrie side were worthy winners 2–0 on the day, and Airdrie won the cup for the first, and only, time in their history before they became defunct in 2002.

Hibs had been handicapped by an early injury to Dunn, but some questioned the sentiment in playing the same team as the year before as some changes might have been of benefit. There were some notable names in the team: Hugh Shaw would go on to manage Hibs in their finest period just after the Second World War, and Jimmy McColl would be his trainer. Jimmy McColl had already won a Scottish Cup winners medal with Celtic against Hibs in 1914 and Jimmy Dunn was to become a Wembley wizard in the 1928 5–1 victory for Scotland over England.

TEAM GREAT BRITAIN

Team Great Britain at the London 2012 Olympics might not have had any Hibernian connections, but this wasn't always the case going back in time. Indeed, in 1948 the last time the Olympics were held in London, there were several involved in the party who had played for Hibs or would play for Hibs in the future.

Back in 1948, a young up-and-coming manager by the name of Matt Busby managed the Olympic squad. Matt had played at Hibs during the Second World War under Willie McCartney, but was now manager of Manchester United where he was to win the European Cup some 20 years later.

In goal was 17-year-old Queen's Park keeper Ronnie Simpson, who had already shown exceptional ability. He was to arrive at Hibs over a decade later and was considered to be a veteran by the time he came to Edinburgh. Jock Stein allowed him to leave Hibs to join Celtic where he was to round off his career in fine style with a European Cup winners medal and his first Scotland Cap at the age of 36, nearly 19 years after his appearance at the Olympics.

In defence was another Queen's Park player, Jim McColl. Jim was neither a future nor former Hibs player – but his father had been. Jimmy McColl senior was the first Hibs player to score 100 league goals and was give the club over 50 years' service. Jim junior is a lifelong Hibs fan.

Finally, another former Hibs player featured – 26-year-old Bob Hardisty who by this time was playing at Darlington. Bob finished as the Team GB top scorer with three goals. History books often overlook his career at Hibs as he guested during the Second World War from his then club Wolverhampton Wanderers. In total he made 19 appearances for Hibs without scoring a single goal. It was at Hibernian that he played alongside the manager, Busby, and it was to be an association that was revived in future years. Hardisty won three successive amateur cup winners medals, before retiring

in 1957. He came out of retirement to help his old friend Matt
Busby in 1958, playing for the Manchester United reserve
team to allow them to fulfil their fixtures.

CUP WINNERS II – SCOTTISH CUP 1901/02

Hibernian won the cup on this occasion on the ground of
their opponents after the original venue, Ibrox was put out of
commission by a disaster which had left 25 dead. Undeterred,
Hibs went on to win the cup.

First round
11 Jan   H   Clyde   2–0 W

Second round
25 Jan   A   Port Glasgow Athletic   5–1 W

Quarter-final
22 Feb   A   Queen's Park   7–1 W

Semi-final
22 Mar   A   Rangers   2–0 W

Final
26 Apr   A   Celtic   1–0 *W
* At Parkhead

Scorer: Andy McGeachan

Team: Harry Rennie, Archie Gray, Bobby Glen, Barney
Breslin, Jimmy Harrower, Alex Robertson, Johnny McCall,
Andy McGeachan, John Divers, Paddy Callaghan, Bobby
Atherton

Appearances

Harry Rennie	5
Bobby Glen	5
Jimmy Harrower	5
Alex Robertson	5
Paddy Callaghan	5
Andy McGeachan	5
Archie Gray	5
John Divers	5
Barnie Breslin	4
Billy McCartney	4
Johnny McCall	4
Bobby Atherton	3

Goals

Andy McGeachan	6
John Divers	6
Paddy Callaghan	2
Billy McCartney	2
Bobby Atherton	1

THE CUP WINNERS' CUP

It's documented that Hibernian have made the semi-finals of the European Cup (now the Champions League), and the Fairs Cup (now the Europa League), but Hibs also made an impact on the other European competition, the European Cup Winners' Cup.

This competition is now defunct, with the last final being played in 1999. Given that the cup was for National Cup winners and Hibs haven't won the national cup since 1902 it's of little surprise that they only entered the competition once, in 1972/73, when they finished cup runners-up to Celtic after losing the Hampden final 6–1 in 1972. Hibs gained entry due to Celtic winning the league and entering the European

Cup instead. Ironically, at this time the holders were Rangers but they were not to defend their title after being banned by UEFA when their fans rioted in Barcelona.

In the first round, Hibs met Sporting Lisbon and in the first leg away from home Hibs performed brilliantly against a very good side to come away with a 2–1 defeat. The match is also significant for the introduction of the purple away colours which were to become commonplace in the 1970s. Hibs dominated the return leg at Easter Road, and a Jimmy O'Rourke hat-trick contributed to a 6–1 thrashing – the biggest defeat suffered by the Portuguese in European competition until that point.

In the second round, Hibs met Albanian side Besa and brushed them aside easily 7–1 in the first leg at Easter Road. Jimmy O'Rourke was again the hat-trick hero, and when Hibs comfortably negotiated the return leg in Albania leaving with a 1–1 draw, a place in the quarter-finals was secured.

It was some months later in March 1973 that the quarter-final took place, and Hibs were drawn at home first to Hajduk Split. A crowd of 28,424 was at Easter Road to see Hibs take a 4–2 advantage thanks to goals from Arthur Duncan and a hat-trick from Alan Gordon. There was an ominous feeling that the away goals conceded could be a barrier to progression, but Hibs had done well to recover from the loss of two key players by this time: John Brownlie was out for the season after a leg break against East Fife and Jimmy O'Rourke was also missing. Youngsters Des Bremner and Tony Higgins deputised – Bremner in particular was a fine player who would go on to lift the European Cup with Aston Villa in 1982.

The same team started the return leg, but it was not to be Hibernian's night as they crashed to a 3–0 defeat with John Blackley scoring an own goal. It remains the last time that Hibs played three rounds in European competition, and also their last appearance in a quarter-final.

The result knocked the stuffing out of Hibernian, and their league title challenge petered out at home. At Ibrox the following Saturday, they lost 1–0 and John Blackley rounded off a miserable week by being sent off. A win would have taken them to within a point of leaders Rangers with a game in hand and just six games remaining.

CUP FINAL ODDITIES

Over the course of Hibernian's history, there have been a number of players who have appeared for the club in cup finals and never appeared again. The first of these was back at the all-Edinburgh Scottish Cup final of 1896. John O'Neill was a left winger who had signed from Linlithgow. He played in a couple of local cup games and friendlies before he was thrown into the team for the final on 14 March. He scored, as Hibernian succumbed to their local rivals 3–1 and it was to be his only competitive appearance in Hibs colours, leaving the club soon afterwards.

In the League Cup final of October 1950, Hibs fielded 23-year-old Jimmy Bradley, who had never played for the club since being signed from Port Glasgow Rangers, in place of the injured Eddie Turnbull. Willie Ormond took up Turnbull's position with Bradley playing in Ormond's normal left-wing slot. Contemporary newspaper reports suggest that this move was not successful – Hibs had seven full internationalists in their team and had been short-priced favourites for success. Bradley was ineffectual and Hibs, for all their quality, struggled to break down the Motherwell defence. Motherwell took the lead with just 15 minutes remaining, and added two more before the final whistle. The post-war team was not to win a national cup trophy. Former Hib Johnny Aitkenhead did though – he had been unable to command a regular place in the post-war Hibs side so he moved on to Motherwell, winning a cup winners medal against his former team-mates.

Bradley, meanwhile, never played for Hibs again and moved on to Third Lanark.

In 2001 Ian Westwater was the goalkeeping coach who served as cover in the event of injuries. As it turned out the talented reserve goalkeeper, Canadian Mike Franks, did not enjoy the luckiest of seasons and Westwater was often called on to the bench as back up for Nick Colgan. Westwater was number two in the final weeks of the season, and sat on the bench in the Scottish Cup final receiving a runners-up medal for his efforts. He never did play a competitive first-team game for Hibs.

FANZINES

Over the years there have been a number of Hibernian fanzines; some have been short-lived while some were active for quite some time. These include *Hibs Monthly*, *Hibees Glasgow Gossip*, *Tanehsh*, *North East Hibernian*, *Hibees Here Hibees There*, *Down the Slope*, *The Proclaimer* and *The Hibernian*.

The longest-running fanzine was *Hibs Monthly*, which evolved into *Mass Hibsteria*. Although it has been dormant for a couple of years a cup final special was back on the streets in 2012 with hopes for a return for the fanzine in the future. Like many clubs, Hibs have found their fanzines difficult to sustain against the more modern internet message forums.

SUMMER CUP 1964

Jock Stein was only to manage Hibs for a short time – in fact just over a year – but in that time he took the struggling squad and brought them to the verge of the league title. Unfortunately, he departed for Celtic before Hibernian's fate could be determined and history records that the league title went elsewhere that season.

Hibernian, however, did win a trophy under his stewardship when they landed the Summer Cup of 1964. Hibs qualified from a group of Hearts, Dunfermline and Falkirk after a play-off and met Kilmarnock in the semi-final. A 4–3 defeat at Rugby Park was wiped out by a 3–0 victory in the second leg at Easter Road. In the two-legged final they met Aberdeen where a 3–2 away defeat was followed by a 2–1 win at Easter Road. This meant a play-off was required and Hibs had to venture to Aberdeen again for a one-off game in September.

Hibs triumphed 3–1, with goals scored by Peter Cormack, Willie Hamilton and Jim Scott. The team was: Willie Wilson, John Fraser, John Parke, Pat Stanton, John McNamee, Jimmy Stevenson, Peter Cormack, Willie Hamilton, Jim Scott, Neil Martin and Eric Stevenson.

This was one of the youngest sides in Hibs' history up to this point – their average age was just 23 years and 37 days old.

SUMMER CUP 1941

1964 wasn't the first time that Hibernian had won the Summer Cup though – the trophy reintroduced in the 1960s had originally been set up during the war years with Hibs victorious in 1941. That year they had come up against Celtic in the first round, triumphing 5–3 at Parkhead. In the second round they had required a play-off against Clyde after the two legs were tied, before knocking out Dumbarton in the semi-final. This brought a 12 July showdown with rivals

Rangers – 17-year-old Gordon Smith was left out, and he related later that is was one of the biggest disappointments of his glittering career. Hibs won 3–2 at Hampden, the goals coming from Bobby Baxter and a brace from Willie Finnegan including one penalty. The Hibernian team that day was: Jimmy Kerr, Davie Shaw, Alex Hall, Matt Busby, Bobby Baxter, Sammy Kean, Bobby Nutley, Willie Finnegan, Arthur Milne, Bobby Combe and Jimmy Caskie. The attendance was 37,200 and Jock Shaw – brother of Hibernian's Davie – lined up for Rangers.

Hibs and Rangers again made the final the following year, but the Edinburgh side were unable to defend the trophy: the game ended goalless, and the teams were also tied on corner kicks gained, 2–2. The decider in this instance was the toss of a coin, and Hibs lost the toss giving Rangers victory. Who says penalty kicks are a cruel way to lose a final?

SOUTHERN LEAGUE CUP 1944

The war years saw some innovations in Scottish football and one of these was the Southern League Cup, which was to evolve into the League Cup that is still played for today. It was introduced in 1941 and gave Hibs their second trophy of the war years under Willie McCartney. It also gave them an element of revenge for their earlier loss in 1942 as their cup final opponents were once again Rangers.

Hibs safely negotiated a group of Third Lanark, Albion Rovers and Morton with 5 wins out of 6 before being drawn to face Clyde in the semi-final. Hibs won this 5–3 at Hampden setting up a final against Rangers again.

The final was a tight affair in front of 63,000 at Hampden, and goalkeeper Jerry Dawson suffered a broken leg which hampered Rangers. The game remained goalless though, but on this occasion Hibs had gained an extra corner over their rivals so triumphed by the margin of 6 corners to 5.

LEGENDS – FRANCK SAUZÉE

Franck Sauzée arrived at Hibs in February 1999 as it was becoming obvious that the club's stay in the second tier of Scottish football was going to be a mercifully brief one. Although not a household name he did have an incredible pedigree having previously played for Marseille, Monaco, Atalanta, Strasbourg and Montpellier, and won French Championships, French Cups as well as the Champions League in 1993 with Marseille. He had also played in the French team that had won the Under-21 championship in 1988 – the core of that team was to go on and win the World Cup in 1998. He had won 39 French caps, scoring 9 goals and had captained the team on 9 occasions. This was a player with real talent, but that's not what makes him a Hibs legend – his desire and commitment to the cause marks him down as a truly extraordinary footballer.

If anyone suspected the 33-year-old was here for one final pay day and an easy ticket, they couldn't have been further from the truth as Franck embraced the 'Heebs' and from his debut at the dilapidated Brockville stadium to his final game against Dundee at Easter Road, he showed a passion and commitment that has rarely been matched since. Hibernian found themselves down to 10 men against their closest rivals for the title on his debut, after Paul Hartley had been sent off but with Sauzée and Alex Marinkov in the side, they ground out the win which extinguished the merest glimmer of hope that Falkirk still had. When he scored his first goal for Hibs, he was booked for his celebration.

Back in the Premier League, or the newfangled SPL as it was now known, Sauzée kept his best performances for the games against Hearts and indeed in 9 games against them as a player and manager he didn't finish on the losing side. He also chipped in with goals on these occasions, such as the fine long-range strike in the millennium derby at Tynecastle in what was Hibs' biggest win there in a generation, or a goal in a 3–1 win at Easter Road that cost him 4 front teeth.

Initially when he arrived at Easter Road he was utilised in the midfield, but at the beginning of 2000/01 manager Alex McLeish made changes to the side and introduced a new 3-5-2 formation with Franck the lynchpin at sweeper. Hibs fans weren't expecting much as star striker Kenny Miller had been allowed to leave for Rangers in a £2m deal, but the season proved to be a revelation with Hibs initially chasing Celtic before falling away late in the season to end up third. They did, however, make the Scottish Cup final, unfortunately losing out to a very good Celtic side who completed the treble. This gave Hibs a return to Europe after nearly 20 years, and a valiant performance nearly gave them the victory before conceding killer goals in extra time. By this time, Sauzée had been subbed through injury and his frustration was evident when he smashed the dugout as he was being substituted.

Including friendlies, Franck played 97 times for Hibs scoring 16 goals – the team never lost a game in which he scored. As a manager he was in charge for just 15 games, winning 1, drawing 6 and losing 8. After leaving Hibs he returned to France where he now does TV work.

THE DRYBROUGH CUP

The Drybrough Cup was a short-lived cup that was held on six occasions in the 1970s. It wasn't open to all teams, just the four highest scoring ones in the top two Scottish Divisions. Hibs didn't enter the first competition, which was won by Aberdeen, but won the next two held in 1972 and 1973. After seven successive victories in the competition they finally succumbed to Rangers in 1974 in the semi-final.

In 1972, Hibernian beat Montrose 3–0 in the first round, before knocking out Rangers in the semi–final, again 3–0. Rangers were of course the holders of the European Cup Winners' Cup. In the final Hibs established a 3-goal lead, but Celtic came back strongly leaving it 3–3 after 90 minutes. Extra time was to prove favourable to Hibs and they emerged 5–3 victors. The Hibs team was: Jim Herriot, John Brownlie, Erich Schaedler, Pat Stanton, Jim Black, John Blackley, Johnny Hamilton (Jimmy O'Rourke), John Hazel, Alan Gordon, Alex Cropley and Arthur Duncan. In front of 49,462, the Hibernian goalscorers were Alan Gordon (2), Arthur Duncan, Jimmy O'Rourke and an own goal from Celtic captain Billy McNeill.

In 1973 Hibernian retained the trophy, this time defeating St Mirren in the first round, before again getting the better of Rangers in the semi-final. Their opponents in the final were Celtic once more and on this occasion it was a much tighter game – goalless going into extra time. There was to be just a single strike to seal the game, and it was Hibs striker Alan Gordon who scored it – in the 119th minute.

The Hibernian team showed some changes from the year before: Jim McArthur, Des Bremner, Erich Schaedler, Pat Stanton, Jim Black, John Blackley, Alex Edwards (Bobby Smith), Tony Higgins, Alan Gordon, Iain Munro (Alex Cropley), Arthur Duncan.

SIR MATT BUSBY

Sir Matt Busby was a Scottish international footballer and manager in the middle of the last century best associated with Manchester United where he is the second longest-serving manager after Sir Alex Ferguson. He played 32 games for Hibs, scoring 5 goals.

Ironically, Matthew Busby began his career at Duntocher Hibs and while he didn't play a peacetime game for Hibs, he was an important part of the wartime team in the early 1940s. This team, under manager Willie McCartney, laid the foundations for the domination that would come after the end of the war and players such as Busby and Alex

Hall were instrumental in helping players such as Bobby Combe and Gordon Smith to emerge and develop. It is to Hibernian's good fortune that they were able to persuade him to 'guest' while he was based at the Army Physical Training Corps in Kelso.

Busby was to be knighted after leading Manchester United to European Cup success in 1968, and in 1975 he wrote the foreword to the book, *100 Years of Hibs*.

As an aside, it's interesting to note the first two Scottish managers to win the European Cup had Hibs connections – Jock Stein in 1967, and Matt Busby in 1968.

CUP WINNERS III – LEAGUE CUP 1972/73

Turnbull's Tornadoes. What can you say about them? In the 12 games that made up this cup-winning campaign, one of the longest in League Cup history, Hibs scored 32 goals conceding 14 and sweeping all before them in splendid fashion.

Interestingly, this was one of the few seasons when the top two in the group qualified for the next round – most years it would just have been the winners, meaning Hibs wouldn't have progressed from the group stages.

They did it the hard way, too, knocking out Rangers and Celtic at Hampden, and I don't think you can overstate just how good this Hibs team was. Rangers were the European Cup Winners' Cup holders and Celtic were in the midst of a nine-in-a-row winning streak and had played and lost in the European Cup final in 1970, just two years before.

Section 2

	P	W	D	L	F	A	Pts
Aberdeen	6	5	0	1	19	5	10
Hibernian	6	5	0	1	14	8	10
Queen of the South	6	2	0	4	5	13	4
Queen's Park	6	0	0	6	4	16	0

12 Aug	H	Queen's Park	4–2 W
16 Aug	A	Aberdeen	4–1 L
19 Aug	H	Queen of the South	3–0 W
23 Aug	H	Aberdeen	2–1 W
26 Aug	A	Queen's Park	1–0 W
30 Aug	A	Queen of the South	3–1 W

Second round (two legs)

| 20 Sep | A | Dundee United | 5–2 W |
| 4 Oct | H | Dundee United | 0–0 D |

Quarter-final (two legs)

| 11 Oct | A | Airdrieonians | 6–2 W |
| 1 Nov | H | Airdrieonians | 4–1 W |

Semi-final

| 22 Nov | N* | Rangers | 1–0 W |

Final

| 9 Dec | N* | Celtic | 2–1 W |

* At Hampden Park

Scorers: Pat Stanton, Jimmy O'Rourke

Team: Jim Herriot, John Brownline, Erich Schaedler, Pat Stanton, Jim Black, John Blackley, Alex Edwards, Jimmy O'Rourke, Alan Gordon, Alex Cropley, Arthur Duncan. Unused sub: John Hamilton

Appearances

John Brownlie	12
Erich Schaedler	12
Pat Stanton	12
Jim Black	12
Arthur Duncan	12

John Blackley	11
Alan Gordon	11
Alex Cropley	11
Jim Herriot	10
Alex Edwards	10
Jimmy O'Rourke	9 + 1
John Hamilton	4 + 1
John Hazel	2
Tony Higgins	2
Bobby Robertson	2

Goals

Jimmy O'Rourke	10
Arthur Duncan	5
John Brownlie	3
Pat Stanton	3
Alan Gordon	3
Alex Cropley	3
Alex Edwards	2
John Hamilton	2
John Blackley	1

HAROLD GOUGH

While Joe Baker was the first Hibernian player to be capped for England, there was another player many years before him who had played for Hibs before going on to represent England later in his career. Goalkeeper Harold Gough played for the club in 1918, while on loan from Sheffield United.

Gough played 19 games in total in a struggling Hibernian side, which took some heavy defeats including a 7–1 reverse at Kilmarnock. This belied the quality of the goalkeeper – he was an FA Cup winner with the Blades in 1915 and was to go on to win an England cap a couple of years after leaving Hibs in 1921. Alas, for Harold his international career was only to last one game as England crashed 3–0 to Scotland at Hampden and he was never selected again. Curiously, on his previous visit to Hampden with Hibs he had also lost 3–0 to Queen's Park.

THE PROFESSIONALS

Hibernian players have come from many professions; indeed legendary chairman Harry Swan was a master baker. Duncan Urquhart, a full-back in the 1930s, had been a butcher prior to starting out in football. It is unknown if any candlestick makers have played for Hibs, though!

Former Defender Colin Murdock is now a trainee lawyer, having completed a law degree during his playing career. Alan Gordon was an accountant, and Hibs have had two junior doctors play for them – curiously both were goalkeepers. Hugh Whyte combined his studies and played in goal for Hibs in the 1970s, before he moved on to Dunfermline where he was also the club doctor. Leslie Skene played a solitary game for Hibs in 1902, when he covered for Harry Rennie who was on international duty with Scotland. Skene would later gain his HM, and was to be capped himself in 1904. He was awarded the Miliary Cross during the First World War.

DRUNK AND DISORDERLY

In September 1935 Hibs crashed to one of their worst ever defeats against rivals Hearts – when the dust had settled at Tynecastle they had been beaten 8–3. The manner of loss was terrible and it became apparent that not one, but two players were hung over – visibly so from the side of the pitch. Duncan Urquhart and Willie Watson had both been sterling servants to the club over a number of years but the management took a dim view and gave them both free transfers and neither played for Hibs again, signing for Aberdeen and Ayr United respectively.

In 2001, Russell Latapy missed a training session and then proceeded to go out for a few drinks with his friend Dwight Yorke. This broke the club's strict 48-hour drinks curfew rule before a match, and he was left out of the game versus Hearts but also never played for the club again and left when his contract expired a few weeks later. To compound the misery he was charged and later convicted of drink driving, and missed the 2001 Scottish Cup final which he had helped to take Hibs to.

Russell moved on to Rangers and Alex McLeish, the manager who had 'dismissed' him from Hibs, later joined him. Unsurprisingly he left Rangers soon after.

CUP WINNERS IV – LEAGUE CUP 1991/92

The team that wouldn't die, Hibernian had emerged from one of the bleakest periods in their history, after surviving the Wallace Mercer takeover and Tom Farmer saving the club from the clutches of David Duff and David Rowland. Not much was expected of the team – the season before had been miserable and there was little funding available to strengthen the squad. This season was different, though, as Hibs had broken their transfer record in order to bring the talented and prolific Keith Wright to the club from Dundee, partly funded by the departure of Paul Wright to St Johnstone. The move paid dividends straight away as Hibs fan Keith scored in every round to ensure that Hibernian lifted the Skol Cup. Keith had been on Hibs' books as a youngster but didn't sign for the club and went on to play for Raith Rovers and Dundee before finding the way to his spiritual home. Hibs only used 15 players to secure the trophy – the unluckiest being Mark McGraw who played in every game up to the semi-final before missing the final through injury. Dave Beaumont, who had only recently joined the club from Luton Town, was an unused substitute in the final and therefore picked up a medal before he had actually played for the team. Beaumont did have quite a pedigree – he had played in a UEFA Cup final for Dundee United prior to moving to England.

Second round
20 Aug   A   Stirling Albion   3–0 W

Third round
27 Aug   A   Kilmarnock   3–2 W

Quarter-final
3 Sep   A   Ayr United   2–0 W

Semi-final
25 Sep   N*   Rangers   1–0 W

Final
27 Oct   N*   Dunfermline Athletic   2–0 W

* At Hampden

Scorers: Tommy McIntyre (pen), Keith Wright

Attendance: 40,377

Team: John Burridge, Willie Miller, Graham Mitchell, Tommy McIntyre, Gordon Hunter, Murdo MacLeod, Mickey Weir, Brian Hamilton, Keith Wright, Gareth Evans, Pat McGinlay. Unused subs: Neil Orr, Dave Beaumont.

Appearances
John Burridge   5
Willie Miller   5
Graham Mitchell   5
Murdo MacLeod   5
Mickey Weir   5

Keith Wright	5
Pat McGinlay	5
Gordon Hunter	5
Tommy McIntyre	4
Brian Hamilton	3 + 2
Mark McGraw	3 + 1
Gareth Evans	2 + 2
Callum Milne	2
Neil Orr	1
David Fellenger	0 + 1

Goals

Keith Wright	5
Pat McGinlay	2
Tommy McIntyre	2
Gareth Evans	1
Murdo MacLeod	1

SUNDAY FOOTBALL

Hibernian first played Sunday football on 6 February 1977 against Partick Thistle. The two clubs decided to play their Scottish Cup tie on the Sunday as opposed to the Monday it was originally scheduled for, to attract a better crowd. The move was successful as over 13,779 watched Hibs win 3–0 with goals from Des Bremner, Ally MacLeod and Bobby Smith. However, the experiment wasn't popular with Tom Hart the then Hibs owner and it was only at the behest of the satellite television companies that Sunday football became the norm. Nor was the experiment popular with the Partick Thistle players who were part-time and bemoaned having their only day off taken up by football duties.

Sunday fixtures are now much more acceptable. In 2000/01 and 2006/07 Hibernian played 12 Sunday games and in the six seasons up to 2011/12 Hibs played a total of 36 games at Easter Road on the Sabbath – an average of 6 games a season.

CHRISTMAS DAY

Although it would be unthinkable nowadays, Christmas Day football used to be a regular fixture in the Scottish League calendar when it fell on a Saturday. The last such game involving Hibs was in 1971 when a crowd of 25,145 turned up to see Hibs go down to Rangers at Easter Road in a 1–0 defeat. The next time that fixtures were scheduled to be played on Christmas Day itself was in 1976 and Hibs opted to bring their game against Ayr United forward to Christmas Eve – only 3,875 turned up to see Hibernian win thanks to an Ayr United own goal. After this the fixtures were dropped altogether and we are unlikely to see a Christmas Day game in the foreseeable future.

Hibernian would have been upset to see the end of the fixture as they had enjoyed an unbeaten run on Christmas Day from losing to Dundee in 1915 until the loss against Rangers in 1971 – a run of seven games.

Christmas Eve fixtures have also gone out of fashion, although Hibs played again on this day in 2011 – the first time since 1977 when they beat Motherwell in a Scottish Premier League game. In 2011 they visited Tannadice in an early kick-off game where they lost 3–1. This date has produced at least two remarkable games in Hibs' history. In 1898, they crashed to their biggest ever league defeat when they lost 10–0 at Ibrox, but on a happier note they got the better of Third Lanark in 1960 by the amazing score of 8–4, despite going a goal behind in the first couple of minutes of the match. Joe Baker scored five, with John Baxter getting a couple and Jim Scott completing the scoring.

NEW YEAR'S DAY

Again, this is another traditional game that is becoming less common, although Hibernian played Hearts in 2011 at Tynecastle, which was the first New Year's Day match since 1998. Hearts won by the only goal of the game in 2011, while back in 1998 goals from Pat McGinlay and Andy Walker gave Hibernian a share of the spoils in a 2–2 draw.

While Hearts have a slight edge in these games, Hibs have also enjoyed their own runs of supremacy. From 1920 until 1934 they went 10 games undefeated in the New Year's Day fixture, winning 6 and drawing 4. They also enjoyed a run from 1968 until 1985 unbeaten, another run of 10 games. Indeed, for the first six games of this run they didn't concede a goal. This run included the game in 1973, when Hibs ran riot at Tynecastle scoring 7 goals without reply.

Although the vast majority of the fixtures have been versus Hearts, Hibs have also played against other teams when the two Edinburgh sides have not shared the same division. In 1983 they lost 2–0 at Pittodrie and in 1981 Hibs saw the New Year in across the border in a 2–0 victory at Berwick Rangers. Prior to that, Hibs visited the now defunct team of St Bernard's for a 1932 derby. Hibs went down that day to their Edinburgh rivals 1–0.

CUP WINNERS V – LEAGUE CUP 2006/07

This cup-winning run is unique in Hibs' history, in that it transcended two managers –Tony Mowbray was in charge for the opening two games of the campaign and John Collins took over from the quarter-final onwards. Hibernian dominated this tournament with convincing wins over all of their opponents. While the Hearts victory is recorded as only 1–0, seldom have Hibs dominated any opponent as much as they did their city rivals that night, and the BBC after the game recorded the possession as being 81:19 per cent in Hibs' favour.

Hibernian were dominant again the final, and once they went ahead the result was never in doubt against a strong Kilmarnock side who were managed by favourite villain Jim Jeffries, the former manager of Hearts. John Collins had recently lost his dad, and the victory was very important to him.

Carrying on a strange tradition at Hibs, Simon Brown picked up a medal without playing in the competition. The much-maligned Zibi Malkowski had been in goals for the first three games in the tournament, before being dropped by John Collins after a disastrous defeat at Tynecastle on Boxing Day. The recently signed youngster Andy McNeil took over for the semi and final, with Brown moving up to the bench.

Second round
22 Aug   H   Peterhead   4–0 W

Third round
20 Sep   H   Gretna   6–0 W

Quarter-final
8 Nov   H   Hearts   1–0 W

Semi-final
31 Jan   N*   St Johnstone   3–1 W (AET, 1–1 at full time)

Final
18 Mar   N** Kilmarnock   5–1 W

*Match played at Tynecastle Park, Edinburgh.

** Match played at Hampden Park, Glasgow.

Scorers: Rob Jones, Abdessalam Benjelloun (2), Steven Fletcher (2).

Team: Andy McNeil, Steven Whittaker (Kevin McCann), David Murphy, Rob Jones, Chris Hogg (Shelton Martis), Scott Brown, Lewis Stevenson, Guillaume Beuzelin, Ivan Sproule (Merouane Zemmama), Steven Fletcher, Abdessalam 'Benji' Benjelloun.
Unused subs: Simon Brown, Michael Stewart.

Appearances

Rob Jones	5
Scott Brown	5
David Murphy	5
Abdessalam Benjelloun	3 + 2
Steven Fletcher	3 + 2
Steven Whittaker	4
Ivan Sproule	4
Shelton Martis	3 + 1
Kevin Thomson	3
Dean Shiels	30
Zibi Malkowski	3
Michael Stewart	2 + 1
Merouane Zemmama	2 + 1
Guillaume Beuzelin	2 + 1
Chris Hogg	2
Chris Killen	2
Andy McNeil	2
Lewis Stevenson	1 + 1
Jay Shields	1 + 1
Jamie McCluskey	0 + 2
Kevin McCann	0 + 2
Stephen Glass	0 + 1

Goals

Abdessalam 'Benji' Benjelloun	5
Steven Fletcher	4
Rob Jones	3
Scott Brown	2
Dean Shiels	2
David Murphy	1
Jamie McCluskey	1

APRIL FOOLS

Traditionally, Hibernian's worst month for football is April when they have their lowest ratio of wins per games played – an average of just over 35 per cent. The best month for Hibs is August where they have a win percentage of just over 49 per cent.

ALL CREATURES GREAT AND SMALL

Jim Herriot was a talented goalkeeper who arrived at Hibs from Durban City in the veteran stages of his career. He was signed by Eddie Turnbull to cover a goalkeeping shortage well into his 32nd year, and he was to perform with distinction during his 93-game Hibs career. Prior to joining Hibs he had accumulated 8 Scotland caps and also a Scottish League cap too. In his time at Hibs he won both the Drybrough Cup and League Cup in 1972, but his tenure was to end when the manager blamed him for the performance in the European Cup Winners' Cup quarter-final against Hajduk Split in Yugoslavia (now Croatia) when Hibs failed to defend a 4–2 advantage from the first leg and went down 3–0 away. Herriot never played for Hibs again, leaving in the close season for St Mirren.

He was also the first member of the 'Turnbull's Tornadoes' to leave as the manager broke up the team as he believed he had better goalkeeping options at the club.

However, that's not how he is best known. His name, James Herriot, was used as a pseudonym by Alf Wight, a veterinary surgeon who had written a series of semi-autobiographical books which became the 'All Creatures Great and Small' series, spawning a popular television series which starred Christopher Timothy. Wight was also a football fan, and chose the name after seeing Herriot excel in a televised match between his then club Birmingham City and Manchester United.

DINO ZOFF

Dino Zoff was an extraordinary goalkeeper between the 1960s and '80s for Italy. He won many honours for both Juventus and Italy, for whom he captained the side that won the 1982 World Cup at the age of 40. He won 112 caps for Italy and holds the record for the longest time at international level without conceding a goal – he went 1,142 minutes between 1972 and 1974.

He probably hasn't forgotten the night he played at Easter Road, though. He visited Edinburgh in November 1967, as part of a Napoli team in the Fairs Cup. Nobody gave Hibs a chance that night as they had lost the first leg in Naples 4–1 the previous week. Hibernian manager Bob Shankly was convinced that Hibs could win not only the tie, but progress and ultimately he was proved right. Napoli, on the other hand were so confident of success that they left their star striker José Altafini at home, thinking that the job had been done in Naples – Altafini had caused the Hibs defence untold problems in that first leg.

In the return at Easter Road, it took just 5 minutes for the Scots to break the deadlock when full-back Bobby Duncan fired a long-range shot past the helpless Zoff. Better was to follow, and Hibernian attacked in wave after wave; Peter Cormack was unlucky not to win a penalty and Stanton was unfortunate to see Zoff keep out an excellent attempt, but on the stroke of half time Hibs went in 2–0 up as Pat Quinn was first to react when a Colin Stein shot came back off the post. Midway through the second half and Hibs scored again through Peter Cormack putting them 3–0 up on the night, and on the verge of qualification through the then newfangled away goals rule. Not that it was to matter, as Hibs added a fourth through Pat Stanton before Colin Stein added a fifth to see Hibs easily home.

In front of an Easter Road crowd of 21,000 the team that cold November night was: Willie Wilson, Bobby Duncan, Joe Davis, Pat Stanton, John Madsen, Allan McGraw, Alex Scott, Pat Quinn, Colin Stein, Peter Cormack, Stevenson.

Zoff, however, was to finish the 1967/68 season on a high as he broke into the Italian team which captured the European Championship in Rome alongside his Napoli colleague Antonio Juliano.

Altafini was to show up later when Hibs drew Juventus in the UEFA Cup of 1973. This time their Italian rivals didn't show the same complacency and Altafini, who had been a member of the 1958 World Cup-winning squad with Brazil alongside Pelé, starred as Hibs crashed 8–2 on aggregate.